Eyewitness
WORLD SERIES

1930s
Cardinals hat

1946 pennant-
winning
Cardinals

Frank Viola

Roberto Clemente
bobble-head doll

1978 Yankees pin

1919 World Series ticket

1915 Athletics uniform

1982 Brewers
pennant

1955 champion Brooklyn Dodgers

Eyewitness
WORLD SERIES

Written by
JAMES BUCKLEY, JR.

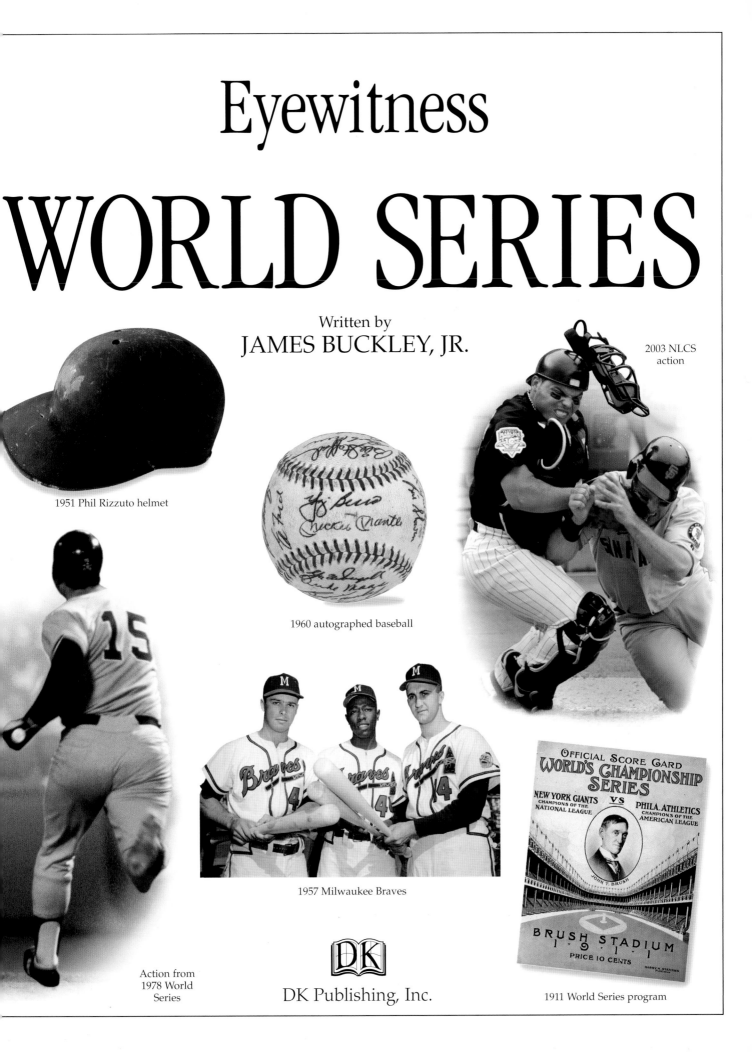

1951 Phil Rizzuto helmet

1960 autographed baseball

2003 NLCS action

1957 Milwaukee Braves

Action from 1978 World Series

DK Publishing, Inc.

1911 World Series program

Reggie Jackson

1978 World Series ball

LONDON, NEW YORK, MELBOURNE,
MUNICH, and DELHI

Project Editor Beth Sutinis
Assistant Managing Art Editor Michelle Baxter
Creative Director Tina Vaughan
Jacket Art Director Dirk Kaufman
Production Manager Chris Avgherinos
DTP Coordinator Milos Orlovic

Produced in partnership and licensed by
Major League Baseball Properties, Inc.
Senior Vice President of Publishing and MLB Photos
Don Hintze

Produced by Shoreline Publishing Group, LLC
President–Editorial Director James Buckley, Jr.
Designer Diana Catherines, Design Design

Published in the United States in 2004 by DK Publishing, Inc.
375 Hudson Street, New York, New York 10014
04 05 06 07 08 10 9 8 7 6 5 4 3 2 1

Copyright © 2004 DK Publishing, Inc.

Text Copyright © 2004 James Buckley, Jr.

DK Publishing, Inc. offers special discounts for bulk purchases for
sales promotions or premiums. Specific, large-quantity needs can be
met with special editions, including personalized covers, excerpts of
existing guides, and corporate imprints. For more information,
contact Special Markets Department, DK Publishing, Inc., 375
Hudson Street, New York, NY 10014
Fax: 800-600-9098.

A catalog record for this book
is available from the Library of Congress

ISBN 0-7566-0256-4 (HC) 0-7566-0255-6 (ALB)

Color reproduction by Colourscan, Singapore
Printed in China by Toppan Printing Co., (Shenzhen) Ltd.

Discover more at

www.dk.com

Frank Viola

1910 glove

Willie Mays

Old World Series trophy

Contents

2003 ALCS action

Before the World Series

BASEBALL AS WE KNOW IT TODAY was "invented" in 1846. Professional teams began play in 1869, but it was not until the 1880s that national championships were played. The National Association (later the National League, or N.L.) became the first pro league in 1871—but they didn't have another league to face in a championship "series" until the birth of the American Association in 1882. Several postseason series were held from 1884 through 1901, when the new American League, or A.L., became a "Major League."

EARLY BALL
Teams in the late 1800s played with crudely made balls such as this. Baseballs were not as hard and were used for much longer periods during games.

TOP TEAM
In 1894, the Baltimore Orioles earned this medal.

EARLY TROPHY
This silver Dauvray Cup was presented to the winner of an annual postseason series between the N.L. and A.A. champs from 1887 to 1890. It was donated by actress Helen Dauvray, who was married to Giants player John M. Ward.

Silver cup with baseball player figures on the handles

Uniform shirt tied with string

CAP ANSON
One of baseball's greatest players, Adrian "Cap" Anson helped the Chicago White Stockings win five N.L. pennants between 1880 and 1886. In 1885, he batted .423 in seven games as the White Stockings defeated the St. Louis Browns in what was then the championship of baseball. Though a sad part of Anson's legacy was his overt racism, his skills on the field were among the best of his era. He was named to the Hall of Fame in 1939.

High-topped leather shoes

FIRST NINE OF THE
CINCINNATI
(RED STOCKINGS) BASE BALL CLUB.

UNCHALLENGED CHAMPIONS
The 1869 Cincinnati Red Stockings, led by captain George Wright (center) were the first pro team. They put together an undefeated season that year, claiming the first pro championship.

ANOTHER KIND OF BALL
The championship Reds pro team sometimes used this type of baseball in their games. The stitches are much flatter and the leather cover has been tanned to a lighter color than the ball at the top of this page.

THE HOOSIER THUNDERBOLT

Few players can say they changed the game. New York Giants pitcher Amos Rusie certainly did. Rusie struck out so many batters that the mound was actually moved back, in 1893, to its present 60 feet, 6 inches. Rusie led the Giants to victory in the 1894 Temple Cup competition.

Figure of player in relief on front of trophy

Knickers-style pants were first used in the 1860s and remain part of the baseball uniform today.

Note the early spelling of the name of the game: "Base Ball."

The National League of Professional Base Ball Clubs

MR. MACK'S MEN

The demise of the American Association in 1882 ended postseason play temporarily. In 1894, a businessman from Pittsburgh named William Temple offered this elegant silver trophy to the winner of the playoff between the first- and second-place finishers in the N.L. The New York Giants won the first Temple Cup in 1894, followed by the Cleveland Spiders in 1895. The Baltimore Orioles won the final two cups in 1896 and 1897. Interest in the cup died out after that, and the trophy now resides in the Baseball Hall of Fame in Cooperstown, New York.

SCORECARD

This colorful scorecard and program from the 1894 Temple Cup competition includes a photo of trophy donor William Temple at bottom left.

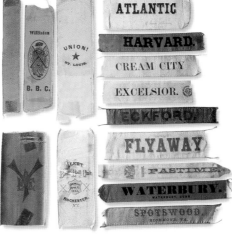

RIBBONS

Tattered now, more than a century later, but prized at the time, these souvenir ribbons represent various pro and amateur teams from the late 1800s. The Atlantics (top ribbon) played in Brooklyn and claimed a national amateur title in 1865.

TWO TALENTS

John M. Ward not only pitched one of the first perfect games, he was a Hall of Fame shortstop and outfielder. He had six RBI in the Giants' 1894 Temple Cup victory. Later he became a top sports lawyer.

John M. Ward, Capt. New York B. B. Club.

Newsboy   NEW YORK.

Heavy wool sweater worn during pregame warmups

MR. ORIOLE

John McGraw helped Baltimore win several titles. Later, as manager, he would have a large effect on future World Series.

The first World Series

THE AMERICAN LEAGUE joined the National League in 1901 as one of two Major Leagues. This soon led the public to call for a postseason series between the two league champions to determine the "world champion." After much discussion, the two leagues agreed on rules for the event. On October 1, 1903, Boston (A.L.) faced Pittsburg (N.L.) in what was known as the World's Series.

HISTORIC DOCUMENT
This contract, signed by the presidents of the two teams, spells out the rules of play and organization for the first World Series, which was the best of nine games.

Pirates owner Barney Dreyfuss

Boston president Henry J. Killilea

FIRST BALL
This is the actual baseball used for the first four innings of the very first World Series game. Hall of Famer Cy Young pitched for Boston. In those days, a baseball might be used for several innings or even a whole game. Today, the average life of a Major League baseball is about seven pitches.

PITTSBURG STAR
That's right: Pittsburg. The Pennsylvania city did not use the final "h" that it uses today. Outfielder Tommy Leach starred for the Pirates during the first Series, knocking in a Series-high seven runs. Key to his success were his four triples, not unusual for an era when home runs were more rare than today.

Wooden bat with handle much less tapered than today's bat handles

Baggy wool pants, held up by leather belt

The B is for Boston, the A for Americans, the nickname of Boston's A.L. team in 1903. They became the Red Sox in 1909.

Leather belt

DOUBLE DUTY
Boston's third baseman, Jimmy Collins, was also the team's manager. Player-managers were not unusual in this era. Collins had two outstanding pitchers at his disposal: Cy Young and Bill Dineen, who won five games between them.

SMILE, GENTLEMEN! PLAYERS PAUSE IN A PREGAME POSE
The two teams (Boston in the front rows) posed together in Boston for this photo before they played Game 8 of their World Series. Led by "Big" Bill Dineen, the Boston club won the clinching game 3–0. The Pirates' pitcher was Deacon Phillippe, who was tossing his fifth game of the Series on only two days' rest.

SERIES DRAWS BIG CROWDS

Before Game 1 of the 1903 Series, huge crowds poured onto the Huntington Avenue Grounds. Though the infield was cleared, fans ringing the outfield remained where they were. Special ground rules were made for balls flying into the crowd, which was numbered at more than 16,000.

KEEPING TRACK

The slip of paper shows the complete story of the business side of Game 1 of the 1903 Series. It lists the total number of people sitting in the grandstand and in the areas behind the plate. Boston, the home team, prepared this report for the visiting Pirates.

Pirates share of ticket sales: $4,060.50

YOUNG, CLEVELAND

Baseball card features hand-colored drawing of Young from his days with Cleveland

THE GREAT CY YOUNG

Boston was blessed with one of the finest pitchers of this or any era. Cy Young played for Boston from 1901 to 1908, leading the A.L. in victories three times.

The Giants' 1904 players are shown in Sporting Life, a popular magazine.

NO SERIES IN 1904

In 1904, the year after the first World Series, the New York Giants refused to play the A.L. champion Boston team and no Series was played. As a snub against the "Junior Circuit," Giants players wore this jersey.

WORLD'S CHAMPIONS

SPORTING LIFE

Heroes and history

I**N THE YEARS BEFORE** World War I, the World Series firmly established itself on the American sports scene. Fans thrilled to all-time great players such as Ty Cobb, Honus Wagner, and Eddie Collins. The N.L.'s Chicago Cubs won two World Series (1907 and 1908), while the A.L.'s Philadelphia Athletics won two (1910 and 1911). The A.L.'s Chicago White Sox of 1906 were known as the "Hitless Wonders" for their ability to win without getting a lot of hits. That was not that unusual for the time. Baseball in this era emphasized defense, great pitching, and bunting.

MATTY WAS MAGIC IN '05
New York Giants pitcher Christy Mathewson wore this sweater during his Hall of Fame career. In the 1905 World Series, he threw three shutouts in five days, striking out 18 and walking only one. His 0.00 ERA remains a Series record.

HALL OF FAME GLOVE
Like most things in baseball, the gear players use has changed since the early days. Unlike gloves of today, the fingers of this glove, used by Mathewson, were not attached and the webbing between thumb and finger was very small.

A CHAMPIONSHIP TEAM
After refusing to play the A.L. champion in 1904, the New York Giants (pictured on a 1905 World Series program) agreed to play in 1905, when they defeated Philadelphia.

OLD-TIME BALLPARK
Crowds were so large at New York's Polo Grounds for the 1905 World Series that they spilled onto the field. Instead of fences, the edges of the outfield (bottom of photo) were formed by a ring of fans. Many fans came to the games in horse-drawn carts and buggies.

HITLESS WONDERS TRY TO HIT
A White Sox batter awaits a pitch from Cubs hurler Jack Pfeister during the 1906 Series. This rare action photo shows how little the game has changed in 100 years.

RESULTS: 1905–1911
1905 New York (N.L.) 4, Phil. (A.L.) 1
1906 Chicago (A.L.) 4, Chicago (N.L.) 2
1907 Chicago (N.L.) 4, Detroit (A.L.) 0#
1908 Chicago (N.L.) 4, Detroit (A.L.) 1
1909 Pittsburgh (N.L.) 4, Detroit (A.L.) 3
1910 Phil. (A.L.) 4, Chicago (N.L.) 1
1911 Phil. (A.L.) 4, New York (N.L.) 2
Game 1 ended in a tie due to darkness

GO CUBS!
Not even Hall of Famer Ty Cobb could lead the Detroit Tigers over the Chicago Cubs in 1907. This scorecard from that World Series shows a team photo of Detroit.

1908: CUBS WIN!
After winning a famous one-game playoff over the Giants for the N.L. pennant, the Chicago Cubs knocked off the Detroit Tigers in the 1908 World Series. This is the scorecard.

THE DUTCHMAN
Honus Wagner helped the Pirates win the 1909 World Series. This baseball card of him has been valued as high as $500,000.

The Athletics used a white elephant as one of their symbols.

THE MIGHTY A'S
Connie Mack would end up leading the Philadelphia Athletics for more than 50 years, longer than any other manager. In 1910, he had his first great success. With the help of star second baseman Eddie Collins, the "Mackmen" defeated the Chicago Cubs in five games to win the world championship.

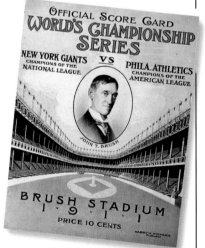

1911 PROGRAM
This program was sold at New York's Brush Stadium (later called the Polo Grounds), named for the Giants' owner, John T. Brush. The Philadelphia Athletics made it two titles in a row as they beat the Giants in six games.

1911 PREGAME POSE
Action photos (like the one on the opposite page) from this era are rare. More common are posed pregame scenes such as the one at left. Players from both teams were on the field for pregame practice, and photographers often got them to stand together. Here the Giants' Rube Marquard, in the all-black uniform the team sported for the Series only, poses with an unidentified member of the Athletics. The man's mitt, however, says he's a catcher.

Padded leather mitt with separate compartment for thumb only; no separate finger holes

CHAMPIONS 1912
RED SOX
WORLD'S SERIES
FENWAY PARK, BOSTON.
Souvenir Biography and Score Book.
Price, 10 Cents

Red Sox's last hurrah

T HE BOSTON RED SOX are one of baseball's most beloved teams. For most of the twentieth century, and into the next, however, they were also one of the most unlucky. Fans today look back on these years, 1912–1918, as among the team's greatest. Boasting a young pitcher named Babe Ruth and an outstanding overall team, Boston won three Series.

BOSTON FANS
The Royal Rooters were the most loyal Red Sox fans in this era.

1912 PROGRAM
A dropped fly ball by Giants outfielder Fred Snodgrass proved to be the key play in the final game of the 1912 Series. Boston took advantage and scored two runs in the bottom of the tenth inning to clinch the win.

Wood won 34 games for Boston in 1912.

1912 MOUND ACES
Red Sox fireballer "Smokey" Joe Wood is on the left, meeting young Giants star Jeff Tesreau, whose 1.96 ERA led the N.L. In the Series, Wood won three games while leading the Sox to the championship.

Reference to "World's Series."

BOSTON VS. NEW YORK
1912 WORLD'S SERIES
FENWAY PARK
RAIN CHECK
GAME 5 3160
Bleacher 50c
In the event that 4½ innings of this game are not played this check is good for succeeding game if presented at the ticket window for redemption.
James McAleer,
President

GIANTS vs. ATHLETICS
Congratulations John! Five Championships in Ten Years!
1913 WORLD'S SERIES

Caption notes the Giants' great record of five N.L. titles in 10 years.

1914'S MIRACLE BRAVES
The Boston Braves (third baseman Charlie Deal is shown) came from last place in July to win the World Series. They knocked off the heavily favored Athletics in a stunning four-game sweep.

PACKED HOUSE
This ticket (check out that price!) let a fan into Game 5 of the 1912 Series at Fenway Park. More than 34,000 people packed the brand-new stadium. Fenway is the only park from 1912 still in use.

1913 PROGRAM
The colonial figure on the left represents the Philadelphia Athletics, shaking the hand of Giants manager John McGraw. The A's knocked off Mighty Mac in five games.

RESULTS: 1912–1918
1912 Boston (A.L.) 4, New York (N.L.) 3*
1913 Philadelphia (A.L.) 4, New York (N.L.) 1
1914 Boston (N.L.) 4, Philadelphia (A.L.) 0
1915 Boston (A.L.) 4, Philadelphia (N.L.) 1
1916 Boston (A.L.) 4, Brooklyn (N.L.) 1
1917 Chicago (A.L.) 4, New York (N.L.) 2
1918 Boston (A.L.) 4, Chicago (N.L.) 2
* One game ended in a tie due to darkness.

The Boston Braves featured all-black uniforms, rare in an era of all-white gear.

PITCHING POWERHOUSE
Pitcher Chief Bender of the Athletics wore this jersey and cap. Bender took part in World Series in 1910, 1911, 1913, and 1914, winning five games as the A's won three titles.

ACTION AT THE PLATE
Philadelphia first baseman Stuffy McInnis scored on this play during Game 1 of the 1914 Series. However, it was the Athletics' only run in a 7–1 loss, the first game of the Braves' four-game sweep. Though McInnis hit .314 for the season, he managed only a .143 average in the Series.

Umpires wore their padded leather chest protectors outside their suits.

1916 RED SOX
From its earliest days, the World Series and its players were used in advertising, such as this button for a brand of beer. This shows the 1916 champion Red Sox, led by pitcher Babe Ruth (top left). Ruth allowed only one run in 14 innings. He won two more games when Boston won it all again in 1918.

Third baseman Larry Gardner knocked in six runs to lead the Red Sox over Brooklyn.

Batboys' uniforms were copies of the players'.

Metal cage mask with padded leather and leather strap

RARE 1916 ACTION PHOTO
Sports photography has come a long way since these early World Series. Few action photos such as this one have survived. Here, Brooklyn catcher Chief Meyers smacks a single during Game 2 of the 1916 Series. Brooklyn's team was known as the Robins, after manager Wilbert Robinson.

Leather and canvas catchers' chest protector

NEED A BAT?
This young man worked as a batboy for the 1917 champion Chicago White Sox. Teams hired batboys at their home parks and usually supplied them to visiting teams. Being a batboy was as exciting then as it is today.

BEFORE THE BAD DAYS
Outfielder Joe Jackson of the White Sox is featured on this sporting-goods catalog. See page 14 for more about his sad story.

MAKING THE CALLS
Though regular season games used two umpires, four umpires were used for World Series games of this era (six are used in today's Series). This umpiring crew from the 1917 World Series included future Hall of Fame ump Bill Klem (holding mask). The man holding the megaphone was the public address announcer. Stadiums did not have loudspeakers then; announcers simply shouted out the starting lineups to the crowd.

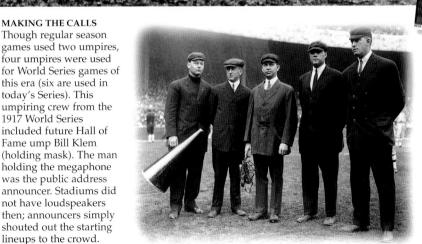

1917 PROGRAM
With World War I looming in Europe, the 1917 Series program featured President Woodrow Wilson.

THE LAST ACT
This program from the 1918 World Series shows a picture of Boston owner Harry Frazee. Only a year later, he sold Babe Ruth to the Yankees, thus "cursing" the Red Sox to this day.

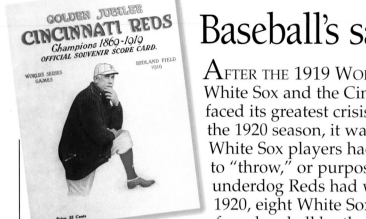

1919 PROGRAM
The Cincinnati Reds celebrated their 50th anniversary as a pro team in 1919. This World Series score card is from Redlands Field, their home park.

Baseball's saddest Series

AFTER THE 1919 WORLD SERIES between the White Sox and the Cincinnati Reds, baseball faced its greatest crisis. By the beginning of the 1920 season, it was suspected that several White Sox players had been paid by gamblers to "throw," or purposely lose, the Series. The underdog Reds had won that Series, and in late 1920, eight White Sox players were banned from baseball by the new commissioner, Kenesaw Mountain Landis. The players had broken baseball's number-one rule: That all players must do their best to win every game.

KEY PLOTTER
Most reports say that White Sox first baseman Chick Gandil, upset at team owner Charles Comiskey's low salaries and poor treatment of players, was a big part of the plan between players and gamblers to throw the Series. Gandil hit .233 for the Series.

Lower grand stand seats were located in the outfield nearest the field.

TAINTED TICKET
Legend says that White Sox pitcher Eddie Cicotte signaled gamblers that the "fix" was in by hitting the Reds leadoff hitter, Morrie Rath, with a pitch at the start of Game 1. Those in the know could then bet heavily on the Reds, confident the White Sox would try to lose the Series.

HOLLYWOOD TREATMENT
In 1988, the movie *Eight Men Out*, based on the book of the same name by Eliot Asinof, was a popular success. The film re-created baseball in 1919 and told the story of the saddest World Series of them all.

WORLD ATTENTION FOR THE SERIES
Massive crowds filled public places like New York's Times Square, above, to read telegraphed reports of ongoing Series games. America was recovering from World War I, and the Series provided a welcome diversion. Also, in the years before radio and TV, this was the only way to see a live game without being at the park.

SAD CASE

White Sox third baseman Buck Weaver tried for years to be reinstated. Though he hit .324 in the Series, Weaver's association with the plotters led to his permanent ban from baseball.

Jackson's .356 career average is second best all-time

SHOELESS JOE'S SHOES

"Shoeless" Joe Jackson got his famous nickname during his minor league days when he had to play part of one game in his bare feet. One of baseball's all-time greatest hitters, he is also one of its most tragic figures. Some experts feel that Jackson did nothing to aid the gamblers during the Series, playing his best. Other evidence, however, including his own testimony, says otherwise. He remains banned from the game to this day, ineligible for the Hall of Fame.

WHAT MIGHT HAVE BEEN

Though he helped Chicago win the 1917 World Series and was such a great hitter that Babe Ruth copied his swing, Joe Jackson had his career cut short in 1920. Following the trial (at which, ironically, all players were acquitted), a young boy supposedly stopped his hero on the courthouse steps and famously said, "Say it ain't so, Joe, say it ain't so!" But it was.

Leather shoes with metal spikes on bottom

THE CHICAGO BLACK SOX

The Chicago White Sox earned the nickame "Black Sox" because their owner often didn't let them wash their uniforms. After 1919, the nickname took on sadder meaning after eight players were implicated in a scandal to throw the World Series, though several denied involvement.

Baseball bounces back

As the 1920s went on, baseball reeled from the aftereffects of the 1919 Black Sox scandal. Fortunately, the sport had a savior. Helped by the new, "lively" version of the baseball itself, put into play in 1920, offense soared. At the center of the run-scoring bonanza was a slightly rotund New York Yankees outfielder named Babe Ruth. Led by Ruth, the Bronx Bombers appeared in six World Series in the decade, winning three of them.

Dodgers manager Wilbert Robinson

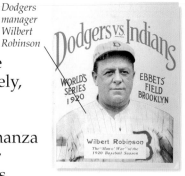

1920: TWO GREAT FEATS
This Dodgers program is from the 1920 Series, which included two amazing firsts. Cleveland's Elmer Smith hit the first grand slam in Series history. Bill Wambsganss of the Indians executed the only unassisted triple play.

1921: HOME SWEET HOME
Only one program was needed for the 1921 Series. That's because it was the only one in which all the games were played in one ballpark: the Polo Grounds, home to the New York Giants and the New York Yankees.

Note the smaller brim style of the day.

KEEPING WARM
New York Giants players wore warmup sweaters such as this during their two-championship run in 1921 and 1922. They defeated the Yankees both times by shutting down the Yanks' powerful bats.

A CONTROVERSIAL TIE GAME
In 1922, the Giants (wearing caps like this one) and Yankees played to one of only two ties in Series history. Game 2 was tied 3-3 when it was called due to darkness. To appease angry fans, Commissioner Landis ordered the game's receipts donated to charity.

EQUIPMENT CHANGE
To increase offense and create a more entertaining game, baseball owners introduced a new ball in 1920. More tightly wound and with a bouncier center, the "lively" ball did its job. This ball has a yellowish cover from a shellac added in later years to preserve it.

Note lack of logos on jerseys of the time.

Cardinals vs. Yankees
for the **Championship** *of the* **World** 1926 **Official Score Card**
Sportsman's Park Saint Louis
Price 25¢

RESULTS: 1920–1929

1920 Cleveland (A.L.) 5, Brooklyn (N.L.) 2*	
1921 New York (N.L.) 5, New York (A.L.) 3*	
1922 New York (N.L.) 4, New York (A.L.) 1#	
1923 New York (A.L.) 4, New York (N.L.) 2	
1924 Washington (A.L.) 4, New York (N.L.) 3	
1925 Pitts. (N.L.) 4, Washington (A.L.) 3	
1926 St. Louis (N.L.) 4, New York (A.L.) 3	
1927 New York (A.L.) 4, Pitts. (N.L.) 0	
1928 New York (A.L.) 4, St. Louis (N.L.) 0	
1929 Philadelphia (A.L.) 4, Chicago (N.L.) 1	

* Best of nine series.

One game ended in a tie due to darkness.

WALTER JOHNSON
In 1924, the 18th season of his Hall of Fame career, Walter "The Big Train" Johnson finally tasted the champagne of a World Series title. Johnson held the Giants scoreless over the final four innings of a 12-inning Game 7. In 1925, he won Games 1 and 4, but his defense let him down in Game 7. The Pirates scored five runs in the seventh and eighth for a come-from-behind victory to earn the Series crown.

GROVER AND THE GOAT
Fans watching Game 7 of the 1926 Series got this colorful scorecard and saw an historic event. The Cardinals' 39-year-old pitcher Grover Cleveland Alexander had pitched a complete-game win the day before—but was summoned from the pen to face the Yankees' Tony Lazzeri with the bases loaded. He struck the young slugger out in a classic confrontation. The Cardinals won the game and the Series.

Yankee uniforms did not have logos or words on the front until 1930.

HALL OF FAME DUO
It's almost unfair that one team should have boasted two such outstanding hitters. From 1923 to 1934, Lou Gehrig and Babe Ruth formed the greatest power-hitting tandem in baseball history. They won their first World Series together in 1927, as the Yankees swamped the Pirates. Gehrig and Ruth combined for 11 RBI and a .357 batting average. They were not the only Yankee sluggers, either. They were joined by Tony Lazzeri and Bob Meusel to form a lineup famously known as "Murderers' Row."

Gold pin given to members of the press to cover the 1927 Series.

Ruth's 48-ounce bat was one of the heaviest ever used in the majors.

SPREADING THE WORD
Though the first Series on radio was aired in 1922, television was years away and millions of fans still relied on newspapers for coverage of the Series. Hundreds of reporters flocked to the Series cities, filing dispatches back to their hometowns. Extra seating was often created in the ballparks to accommodate the overflow press crew, who were given tickets like this one to get in.

Thick wool stirrup socks

A SERIES ROUT
The 1928 World Series (program at right) was a showcase for the Yankees' one-two punch of Ruth and Gehrig. The Bambino hit an astonishing .625, with three home runs. Gehrig was just behind at .545, but he had four homers along with nine RBI. Considering that it was the team's second straight sweep, that's a lot of damage in four games.

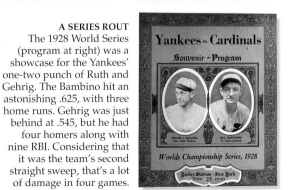

MR. MACK'S MEN
The button at left proclaims the Chicago Cubs "champions," but that was only for winning the 1929 N.L. pennant. In the World Series, they lost to the Connie Mack-led Philadelphia A's, one of the best teams of all time. The program above shows Mack and Cubs skipper Joe McCarthy.

The Yankees roll on

THE 1930S BEGAN WITH A DASH of Pepper but wound up with a four-season blast of Yankees power. St. Louis outfielder Pepper Martin almost singlehandedly won the 1931 Series, but it was a deep Yankees lineup that helped that club win four straight championships from 1936 through 1939. They were the first team to win first three and then four titles in a row. The decade also featured World Series performances by a host of future Hall of Fame players.

MOVIE STAR MEETS THE CHAMPS
The 1930 Philadelphia Athletics played host to comedian Joe E. Brown (holding hat) before a World Series game against St. Louis. Longtime A's manager Connie Mack is to Brown's right.

Charlie Root pitched 16 of his 17 Major League seasons with the Chicago Cubs.

BUY THE BABE!
By the early 1930s, Babe Ruth was a superstar on the field and a popular product spokesman off it (above). With his home-run performances in the 1932 World Series, he became an even bigger legend.

On-deck hitter Lefty Gomez, also the winning pitcher in the game.

ROOT OF THE ISSUE
Chicago pitcher Charlie Root served up a home-run pitch to Babe Ruth in Game 3 of the 1932 Series. No one knows if Babe actually pointed to the outfield seats before hitting the homer right into them.

Hubbell was famous for his high leg kick during his delivery.

RESULTS: 1930–1939

1930 Philadelphia (A.L.) 4, St. Louis (N.L.) 2

1931 St. Louis (N.L.) 4, Philadelphia (A.L.) 3

1932 New York (A.L.) 4, Chicago (N.L.) 0

1933 New York (N.L.) 4, Washington (A.L.) 1

1934 St. Louis (N.L.) 4, Detroit (A.L.) 3

1935 Detroit (A.L.) 4, Chicago (N.L.) 2

1936 New York (A.L.) 4, New York (N.L.) 2

1937 New York (A.L.) 4, New York (N.L.) 1

1938 New York (A.L.) 4, Chicago (N.L.) 0

1939 New York (A.L.) 4, Cincinnati (N.L.) 0

1933 STAR
Though the Washington Senators boasted five hitters who had topped .295 during the season, the Giants shut them down in the Series, led by lefty Carl Hubbell, who won two games and allowed no earned runs.

Hubbell's best pitch was a screwball.

IN 1934, DIZZY WAS DAZZLING

St. Louis pitcher Dizzy Dean wore this jersey during the 1934 season in which he won 30 games. "Ol' Diz" kept it up in the World Series, winning two games, striking out 17, and helping the Cardinals clinch the championship with a shutout performance in their 11–0 Game 7 victory.

This famous logo showing two cardinals on a bat debuted in 1922.

Player's name sewn on shirt

SKYLINE SLUGGERS

This program from the Yankees' 1936 triumph over the Giants features a buffalo-head nickel. This was the first Subway Series between two New York teams. At the time of the Series, a ride on the city subway cost five cents—that's why the program features a nickel.

PINSTRIPE PITCHER

The Yankees often outslugged their World Series opponents, but the club also boasted great pitching. The ace was righthander Red Ruffing, who won four games and allowed only four earned runs from 1937–1939.

TONY TOUCHES 'EM ALL IN 1937

While Babe Ruth and Lou Gehrig got most of the headlines, the Yankees boasted other sluggers. Second baseman Tony Lazzeri, here scoring after a Game 1 homer in 1937, was part of six Yankees World Series clubs.

This card shows Gehrig at practice, wearing this glove.

SWEET LOU

The Yankees' great first baseman Lou Gehrig, who hit .361 with 10 homers in Series play, wore this glove during his Hall of Fame career, which came to a poignant end in 1939.

War can't stop the Series

SOON AFTER AMERICA ENTERED WORLD WAR II in 1941, President Franklin Roosevelt asked baseball to keep playing to help support people at home working hard on the war effort. Though many players left to serve in the armed forces, the games went on, as did the World Series. The absence of some stars helped lesser teams like the Browns finally win a championship (1944). However, when the war was over and the top players returned, order was restored and the Yankees found themselves once again atop the baseball world.

The 1944 Series was the only time two teams shared a home city other than New York.

Pocket was formed not at factory but by catching pitch after pitch.

WARTIME PROGRAM
By the 1942 World Series, America had been involved in World War II for nearly a year. Baseball contributed to the war effort by encouraging fans to buy "war bonds" to help support troops. This 1942 program shows a young player doing his part by buying fundraising stamps.

Preprinted tickets did not show actual team names.

1945 TICKET
The Cubs won this game at Detroit, but the Tigers turned the tables, winning Game 7 in Chicago.

1941'S MITT MISTAKE
Dodgers' catcher Mickey Owen was wearing this mitt when he made a Series-turning mistake. He let a third strike slip by him that would have ended Game 3. Instead, the Yankees rallied to win the game, and later the Series.

RESULTS: 1940–1949

1940 Cincinnati (N.L.) 4, Detroit (A.L.) 3
1941 New York (A.L.) 4, Brooklyn (N.L.) 1
1942 St. Louis (N.L.) 4, New York (A.L.) 1
1943 New York (A.L.) 4, St. Louis (N.L.) 1
1944 St. Louis (N.L.) 4, St. Louis (A.L.) 2
1945 Detroit (A.L.) 4, Chicago (N.L.) 3
1946 St. Louis (N.L.) 4, Boston (A.L.) 3
1947 New York (A.L.) 4, Brooklyn (N.L.) 3
1948 Cleveland (A.L.) 4, Boston (N.L.) 2
1949 New York (A.L.) 4, Brooklyn (N.L.) 1

GUESS WHAT YEAR THEY WON THE N.L. PENNANT?
Four Cardinals flipped their jerseys around to celebrate winning the N.L. pennant and a spot in the World Series. They are third baseman Whitey Kurowski, outfielder Enos Slaughter, shortstop Marty Marion, and future Hall of Fame outfielder Stan Musial.

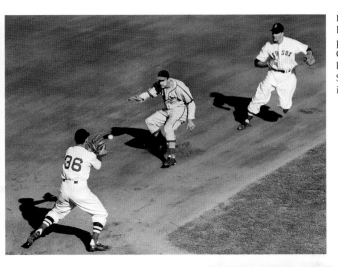

IN A PICKLE IN 1946
Ballet or baseball? Two Red Sox players have Stan Musial of the Cardinals surrounded on the basepath during this 1946 World Series game. St. Louis beat Boston in an exciting seven-game series.

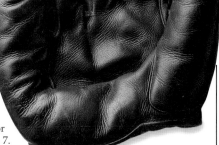

GREAT 1947 CATCH
In Game 6 of the 1947 Series, Dodgers outfielder Al Gionfriddo, using this glove, made an amazing catch of a near-homer by Joe DiMaggio. It saved the game for Brooklyn, but the Yanks won Game 7.

COOKIE COMES THROUGH
In Game 5 of the 1947 Series, Dodgers pinch-hitter Cookie Lavagetto is shown here stroking one of the most famous hits in World Series history. His two-out single in the bottom of the ninth knocked in two runs, which not only won the game for Brooklyn, but also broke up Yankees pitcher Bill Bevens' bid for what would have been the first no-hitter in Series history.

PROGRAM...GET YER PROGRAM!
Though only fifty cents at the time, programs such as these being sold at Yankee Stadium in 1947 are among the most popular collectible items from old World Series.

Ebbets Field was named for the team's former owner.

HOME SWEET HOME
The Dodgers' home ballpark was much-beloved Ebbets Field. This ticket is from Game 5 there in 1947.

RAPID ROBERT
Though Hall of Fame fireballer Bob Feller was 0–2 in the 1948 World Series (fellow ace Bob Lemon was 2–0), the Cleveland Indians overcame the Red Sox to win their first world title since 1920.

Feller pitched no-hitters before and after WWII.

New York, New York

THOUGH THE YANKEES CONTINUED their World Series success in the 1950s, they found competition right in the neighborhood. Of the 20 spots for teams in the Series that decade, 15 went to teams from New York City. Only in 1959 was the city shut out of the Series (and even then, the winner was the Dodgers, who had moved from Brooklyn to Los Angeles). New York fans had a great ten years!

THE SCOOTER'S LID
Yankees shortstop Phil "Scooter" Rizzuto was the unexpected A.L. Most Valuable Player for the 1950 season. On a team of superstars, his steady play helped the Yanks win their second straight World Series— during which Rizzuto wore this batting helmet.

YANKS WIN AGAIN
After winning the 1951 N.L. pennant on Bobby Thomson's famous playoff home run (see page 60), the New York Giants couldn't overcome their crosstown rivals in the championship. The Yankees won their third straight Series, becoming the first team ever to do so.

RESULTS, 1950–1959

1950	New York (A.L.) 4, Philadelphia (N.L.) 0
1951	New York (A.L.) 4, New York (N.L.) 2
1952	New York (A.L.) 4, Brooklyn (N.L.) 3
1953	New York (A.L.) 4, Brooklyn (N.L.) 2
1954	New York (N.L.) 4, Cleveland (A.L.) 0
1955	Brooklyn (N.L.) 4, New York (A.L.) 3
1956	New York (A.L.) 4, Brooklyn (N.L.) 3
1957	Milwaukee (N.L.) 4, New York (A.L.) 3
1958	New York (A.L.) 4, Milwaukee (N.L.) 3
1959	Los Angeles (N.L.) 4, Chicago (A.L.) 2

Autographed by manager Leo Durocher and outfielder Willie Mays

THE SAY HEY KID AND THE LIP
While the Yankees were the big name in town, in 1954, the New York Giants of the N.L. were the champs. This ball was signed by manager Leo "The Lip" Durocher, star outfielder Willie "Say Hey Kid" Mays, and the rest of the Giants.

Home plate umpires of this time held a thick pad that covered their chest and stomach.

A CLASSIC BASEBALL DUST-UP
Umpire Charles Barry makes the out call, Yankees catcher Yogi Berra makes the tag, and Philadelphia outfielder Granny Hamner makes the cloud of dust in this play at the plate from Game 4 of the 1950 World Series. Philadelphia, known as the "Whiz Kids," was making its first Series appearance since 1915.

Phillies shortstop Granny Hamner led his team with a .429 average, but Philly was swept.

Yogi Berra played in more World Series games (75) than any other player in history.

A Perfect Game

Before Game 5 of the 1956 World Series, Yankees manager Casey Stengel left a ball in the baseball cleats of pitcher Don Larsen, meaning Larsen would be the starter that day. It was a surprise move by the wily old skipper. Larsen had lasted less than two innings of Game 2 just three days earlier. But Stengel made the right choice. By not allowing a single Brooklyn Dodgers player to reach base, Don Larsen threw the first and only perfect game in World Series history. New York won 2–0.

A PERFECT PAIR
Shown here are the hat that Don Larsen wore during his perfect game and the catcher's mitt used by Yogi Berra of the Yankees. The ball-strike indicator was used by home plate ump Babe Pinelli.

Count shows 2 and 2

OUR MAN MAYS
Willie Mays was one of the greatest all-around players in baseball history. He helped the Giants win the 1954 World Series with his bat and with his glove.

THE CATCH
Ask any baseball fan to name the greatest catch in history and most will come up with the one that Willie Mays made in Game 1 of the 1954 Series (shown at right). On a long drive hit by Cleveland's Vic Wertz, Mays raced back and caught the ball while facing away from the infield. He then whirled and made a huge throw that kept base runners from scoring. It has become the most famous catch of all time.

LUCKY DUCAT
More than 64,000 people took home this valuable souvenir, a ticket from the most amazing game ever pitched in baseball history.

A JOURNEYMAN
Other than his spectacular perfect game, Don Larsen put together a rather unspectacular Major League career. In 14 seasons, he fashioned an 81–91 career record for eight teams. Larsen has said since that he thinks about his perfect game every day of his life. No one else has even come close to matching his feat.

Jersey worn by Chicago shortstop Luis Aparicio

GO-GO SOX
Chicago's speedy and exciting team was nicknamed the "Go-Go Sox" during the 1959 season. But in the World Series against the Dodgers, they were the Stop-Stop Sox. L.A. won the title in six games.

THE BRAVES BREAK THE STRING
In 1957 and 1958, the Milwaukee Braves finally broke up New York City's hold on the World Series. Led by slugging third baseman Eddie Mathews, future home-run king Hank Aaron, and third baseman Frank Torre, the Braves beat the Yanks twice.

A GREAT YEAR
Dodgers manager Walter Alston (top) and Yankees skipper Casey Stengel are on this 1955 Series program.

Next year finally comes

THE BROOKLYN DODGERS had appeared in seven World Series before 1955. They had lost them all. To make matters worse, they had lost the last five of them to their crosstown rivals, the New York Yankees. Today Brooklyn is a borough of New York. But it used to be a separate city, and it had then (and still has) its own identity. It loved its Dodgers, known as "Da Bums," with a fierce passion. Finally, in 1955, Brooklyn's disappointment ended; after years of "wait till next year," next year finally came.

CAMPY
The heart and soul of the Brooklyn team was catcher Roy Campanella. He wore this jersey during his Hall of Fame career. Sadly, "Campy" was seriously injured in a car accident following the 1958 season.

DUKE SNIDER outfield BROOKLYN DODGERS

AN ALL-AROUND TALENTED TEAM
The Dodgers' pitching staff (left) was anchored by Don Newcombe and Johnny Podres. Outfielder Duke Snider (above) smacked 42 homers in 1955.

A SERIES-SAVING CATCH
Every eye in Ebbets Field is on Dodgers outfielder Sandy Amoros as he snags this long drive by Yogi Berra. Amoros's catch prevented the Yankees from scoring and helped Brooklyn win its first World Series.

HE'S IN THERE!
Amoros helped on the basepaths, too, using his great speed to slide in ahead of the tag of Yogi Berra (8), while Dodgers shortstop and captain Pee Wee Reese looked on. This action was from Game 4 of the Series, which was a nail-biter that went down to a thrilling Game 7.

THAT CHAMPIONSHIP SEASON
The members of this 1955 Brooklyn Dodgers World Series championship team, in the team photo at left, became instant and permanent heroes in Brooklyn. The Dodgers boasted the most loyal and long-suffering fans in baseball. Those fans' hopes finally came true in 1955 after years of close calls.

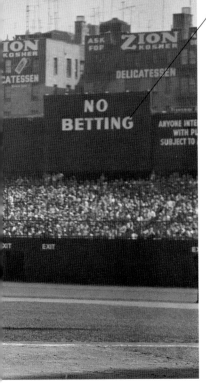

Check out the ads on the outfield walls, and the huge No Betting sign.

TWO FOR THE ROAD
In the victorious Dodgers' locker room following Game 7, team owner Walter O'Malley embraced manager Walter Alston. Though his team had finally earned its long-hoped-for championship, O'Malley was already working toward a sad day for all Dodgers fans. In 1957, he announced that the team would leave Brooklyn and move to Los Angeles. There are some people who say that Brooklyn has never been the same since. But they can look back to 1955 and remember a fantastic year.

GETTING IT STARTED
On the mound in front of more than 63,000 fans at Yankee Stadium, New York's Whitey Ford fires in a pitch during Game 1. Though Ford would give up five runs in the game, the Yanks scored six and won by one run. Yankee Stadium in 1955 did not have its huge outfield facade.

1960: What a show!

ANYONE LOOKING AT THE STATS from this 1960 World Series between the New York Yankees and Pittsburgh Pirates would probably conclude that the Yankees had won big. They scored 55 runs to Pittsburgh's 27. They had 91 hits to Pittsburgh's 60. New York pitchers had an ERA of 3.54 for the seven games, while Pittsburgh hurlers gave up more than seven runs per game. But thanks to good timing, one solid starter in Vern Law (two victories), and one stunning, amazing, unprecedented swing from the player perhaps least likely to produce it, the Pirates were indeed the 1960 champs.

1960 PRESS PIN
Yankees manager Casey Stengel (shown on this press pin) led his team to 10 pennants and seven World Series titles in 12 years, but 1960 was his last with the Yanks.

1960 "FAKE" TICKET
Because teams had to print tickets in advance, some teams who had a shot at the Series were stuck with tickets for games that didn't exist. This un-needed ticket is for Game 4 for the Chicago White Sox.

MICK THE MASHER
Switch-hitting slugger Mickey Mantle was a big part of the Yankees' powerhouse attack during the 1960 regular season, leading the A.L. with 40 homers. He kept up his slugging ways during the Series against Pittsburgh, batting .400, hitting three homers, and knocking in 11 runs.

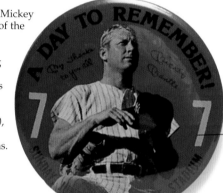

YANKEES ACE WHITEY FORD
Whitey Ford was the linchpin of the Yankees' great pitching staff in the 1950s and 1960s. He holds World Series records for most wins (10), including his mark of 2–0 with a 0.00 ERA in 1960.

Yankees fans could take home these souvenir buttons of two of their heroes.

Baseball helmets in 1960 did not have ear flaps.

MARIS THE MASHER
Rightfielder Roger Maris was the MVP during the 1960 regular season while leading the A.L. with 119 RBI and a .581 slugging percentage. In the Series, he contributed the Yankees' offensive attack with a pair of home runs.

Mazeroski's infielders' glove, smaller than other fielders use

FINDING A HOME IN THE HALL
The Baseball Hall of Fame in Cooperstown, New York, is the home of much of baseball's most famous memorabilia. On this plaque is the bat (since bronzed) used by Bill Mazeroski (see photos at right) used to hit his famous homer. It's shown with the helmet he wore in the game, as well as the glove the top-fielding second baseman used during the 1960 World Series.

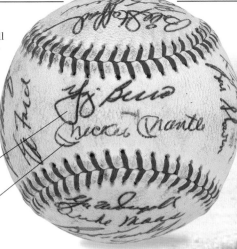

START THE PARTY IN PITTSBURGH!
A huge crowd of fans and players waited for Bill Mazeroski as he made his way toward home plate with the winning run. It was the first time in World Series history that a player had hit a home run to win the Series in the final at-bat. Maz had hit only 11 homers that season and averaged only eight per season in his career.

Scoreboard shows line score of game with blank for bottom of the ninth.

THE GAME AND SERIES WINNING HIT
After the Yankees tied Game 7 with two runs in the top of the ninth, Pittsburgh second baseman Bill Mazeroski stepped to the plate against the Yankees' Ralph Terry. To the amazement of Pirates fans, Mazeroski hit Terry's second pitch (shown here) over the left-field wall for a Series-winning homer!

WORLD SERIES 1962
Yankee Stadium

NEW YORK
YANKEES
vs
SAN FRANCISCO
GIANTS

62

1962 PROGRAM
Though it took seven games, the Yankees won their second straight world title in 1962 by defeating the San Francisco Giants.

Pitchers rule!

THE 1960S HAD BEGUN WITH a home-run blast, but pitching proved to be dominant in the rest of the decade. The St. Louis Cardinals made three Series appearances, led by ace Bob Gibson. The Dodgers' starters, including Sandy Koufax and Don Drysdale, led them to three Series as well. In 1968, 31-game winner Denny McLain and crafty lefty Mickey Lolich took the Tigers to the top. Tom Seaver, Jerry Koosman, and the Mets rounded out a pitching-powered decade.

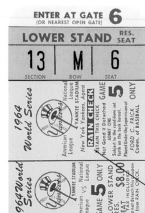

ENTER AT GATE **6**
(OR NEAREST OPEN GATE)

LOWER STAND | RES. SEAT

13 | **M** | **6**
SECTION | ROW | SEAT

1964 World Series

GAME **5** ONLY

LOWER STAND RES. SEAT. $8.00

LAST FOR A WHILE
The Yankees' run of championship seasons ended in 1964. They lost this Game 5 at New York 5–2 to fall behind the St. Louis Cardinals in a Series that St. Louis won in seven games. It was the Yanks' last visit to the Series until 1977.

A rain check is kept by fans in case a game is called for weather.

DE-PRESS-ING
Like the ticket on page 26, this pin was created and then never used. The Phillies' final-week collapse kept them from reaching the World Series, leaving pins like these unused.

WORLD SERIES 64 Phillies PRESS

Pin shows Phillies cap

Koufax is wearing a nylon pitchers' warm-up shirt.

THE BEST EVER?
Was Dodgers lefty Sandy Koufax the best pitcher ever? Some people think so, and his 1961–1966 record of 129–34 and five N.L. ERA titles is good evidence. In the 1965 World Series against the Minnesota Twins, Koufax was brilliant, winning two games while striking out 29 and allowing only 13 hits in 24 innings.

RESULTS: 1961–1969

1961 New York (A.L.) 4, Cincinnati (N.L.) 1

1962 New York (A.L.) 4, San Francisco (N.L.) 3

1963 Los Angeles (N.L.) 4, New York (A.L.) 0

1964 St. Louis (N.L.) 4, New York (A.L.) 3

1965 Los Angeles (N.L.) 4, Minnesota (A.L.) 3

1966 Baltimore (A.L.) 4, Los Angeles (N.L.) 0

1967 St. Louis (N.L.) 4, Boston (A.L.) 3

1968 Detroit (A.L.) 4, St. Louis (N.L.) 3

1969 New York (N.L.) 4, Baltimore (A.L.) 1

St. Louis shortstop Dick Groat

YANKEES FLOP
Mickey Mantle was on the tail end of a great career in the 1964 World Series. The Yankees lost to the Cardinals, but The Mick had three homers to run his career total in the Series to 18, still the most ever. But on this play, the formerly speedy Mantle was picked off second base.

George Scott
(5) greets Yaz
after a homer.

IMPOSSIBLE DREAM
The 1967 Boston Red
Sox, led by Triple
Crown winner Carl
Yastrzemski (right),
stunned the baseball
world by winning
the A.L. pennant.
However, they lost to
St. Louis in a thrilling
seven-game Series.

NEW YORK: DANCING IN THE STREETS
The 1969 New York Mets' surprising World
Series triumph set off a big celebration in New
York City. In the downtown financial
district, fans littered the streets with paper
and confetti, inspiring these two
businessmen to do a victory dance!

THE AMAZIN' METS
The New York Mets franchise
was only seven years old in
1969, and it had been one of
baseball's worst teams. Only
two years earlier, they had
lost 101 games. But it all came
together in 1969. They won
the first-ever N.L.
Championship Series
(page 60) and then
stunned the
powerful Orioles
to win it all in
five games.

Game 5 winning
pitcher Jerry Koosman
of the Mets leaps into
the arms of catcher
Jerry Grote to celebrate
the Mets' triumph.

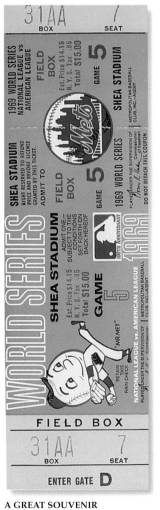

A GREAT SOUVENIR
New York fans treasure ticket
stubs like this one for the final
game of the 1969 Series. At the
bottom, it features the team
mascot, Mr. Met.

Oakland "threepeats"

BEFORE THE GREEN-AND-GOLD, mustachioed, wild-and-crazy Oakland A's of the early 1970s came along, no team other than the New York Yankees had strung together three straight World Series titles (and the Yanks had made it to five straight). But colorful owner Charlie O. Finley put together a team that combined great pitching with clutch power hitting to dominate baseball. Before the A's pulled off their threepeat, the Series saw one of the greatest defensive displays ever, along with what would turn out to be the swan song of one of the game's most beloved players. Then Oakland swung into action. Their players' personalities were almost as colorful as their uniforms.

Robinson played for Baltimore for 23 years.

HOT CORNER MAGIC
In the 1970 Series, Baltimore third baseman Brooks Robinson almost single-handedly (or single-gloved-ly) won it for his team. Brooksie made several spectacular plays against the hard-hitting Reds to back up the O's top-notch pitchers.

RESULTS: 1970–1974

1970 Baltimore (A.L.) 4, Cincinnati (N.L.) 1

1971 Pittsburgh (N.L.) 4, Baltimore (A.L.) 3

1972 Oakland (A.L.) 4, Cincinnati (N.L.) 3

1973 Oakland (A.L.) 4, New York (N.L.) 3

1974 Oakland (A.L.) 4, Los Angeles (N.L.) 1

Cincinnati's Hall of Fame catcher Johnny Bench

MR. BEISBOL
This bobble-head doll honors Pittsburgh's Hall of Fame outfielder Roberto Clemente, MVP of the 1971 World Series. In helping the Pirates defeat Baltimore in seven games, Clemente batted .414 with two homers and several awesome defensive plays. Sadly, this Puerto Rican hero was killed in a plane crash shortly after the 1972 season while delivering relief supplies to earthquake victims in Nicaragua.

WHAT A START!
Though he hit only five homers all season, catcher Gene Tenace opened the 1972 World Series with homers in his first two at-bats (a Series first). He went on to hit two more and collect a total of nine RBI as Oakland knocked off Cincinnati in an exciting seven-game Series. Six of the seven games were decided by one run, including Oakland's 3–2 win in Game 7, which Tenace clinched with a two-run double. The surprise star was the Series MVP.

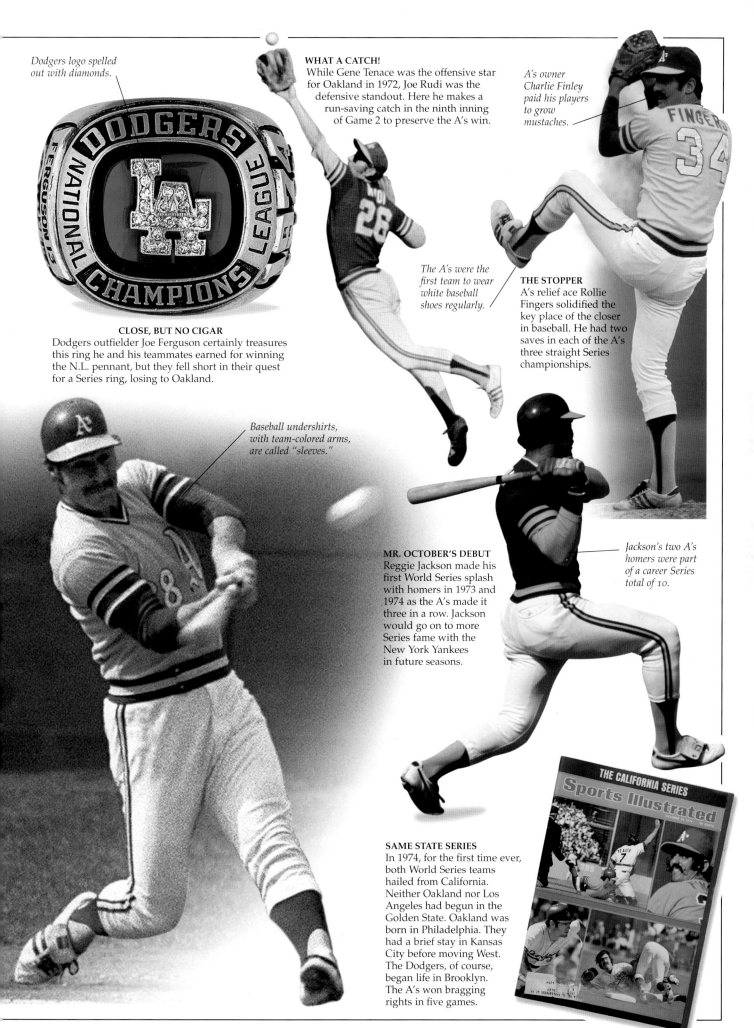

Dodgers logo spelled out with diamonds.

WHAT A CATCH!
While Gene Tenace was the offensive star for Oakland in 1972, Joe Rudi was the defensive standout. Here he makes a run-saving catch in the ninth inning of Game 2 to preserve the A's win.

A's owner Charlie Finley paid his players to grow mustaches.

The A's were the first team to wear white baseball shoes regularly.

THE STOPPER
A's relief ace Rollie Fingers solidified the key place of the closer in baseball. He had two saves in each of the A's three straight Series championships.

CLOSE, BUT NO CIGAR
Dodgers outfielder Joe Ferguson certainly treasures this ring he and his teammates earned for winning the N.L. pennant, but they fell short in their quest for a Series ring, losing to Oakland.

Baseball undershirts, with team-colored arms, are called "sleeves."

MR. OCTOBER'S DEBUT
Reggie Jackson made his first World Series splash with homers in 1973 and 1974 as the A's made it three in a row. Jackson would go on to more Series fame with the New York Yankees in future seasons.

Jackson's two A's homers were part of a career Series total of 10.

SAME STATE SERIES
In 1974, for the first time ever, both World Series teams hailed from California. Neither Oakland nor Los Angeles had begun in the Golden State. Oakland was born in Philadelphia. They had a brief stay in Kansas City before moving West. The Dodgers, of course, began life in Brooklyn. The A's won bragging rights in five games.

THE CALIFORNIA SERIES
Sports Illustrated

The best Series ever?

How good was Game 6 of the 1975 World Series? Stepping to the plate in the ninth inning of the tie game, Cincinnati's Pete Rose turned to Boston catcher Carlton Fisk and remarked, "Boy, this is some kind of game, isn't it?" Pete wasn't alone in thinking that. A Series filled with wild plays, stunning homers, and big stars has gone down in history as perhaps the best ever. Red Sox fans might not agree!

GEM OF A GAME
This ticket let a lucky fan see a memorable Game 6 at Fenway Park. Boston's Bernie Carbo tied the game at 6–6 with a three-run pinch homer, and Dwight Evans's catch took away a Cincy homer before Fisk won it.

BIG RED MACHINE
This charm honors the Reds' 1975 World Series appearance, the first of two straight for a club called The Big Red Machine for their powerful offensive attack that featured four future Hall of Famers.

JUST SAY FISK
Ask real baseball fans what Carlton Fisk means and they'll say: Game 6 homer. Fisk's 12th-inning blast off the left-field foul pole (cameras caught him waving at the ball as it flew) broke a 6–6 tie and won the game.

Bench's mitt featured the newer built-in pocket.

LYNN'S REMARKABLE SEASON
Centerfielder Fred Lynn had one of the most amazing rookie seasons ever in 1975. With 105 RBI and a .331 average, he became the first player to be named both Rookie of the Year and MVP in the same season. In the Series, Lynn made several great defensive plays, and had a homer and five RBI.

ALL-AROUND STAR
Reds catcher Johnny Bench was among the first to use a mitt like this one, which allowed him to catch one-handed. Bench combined this defensive skill with the best bat for a catcher since Yogi Berra. He had a homer and four RBI in the Series.

Fisk made the tag after taking the throw from left fielder Juan Beniquez.

YER OUTTA THERE!
Carlton Fisk tags out Pete Rose in a close play at home in the first inning of Game 3 at Cincinnati. The Reds went on to win that game 6–2 to take a three-games-to-two lead, setting up the drama of Game 6. Rose, for his part, batted .370 for the Series, the best mark of his six Fall Classic appearances.

DANCE OF THE WINNING REDS
While Game 6 ended with a dramatic Red Sox win, the Fenway faithful had to watch the Reds do the ultimate victory dance. The Red Sox blew a 3–0 lead, watching the Reds storm back to win the game 4–3 and the Series.

First baseman Tony Perez' two-run homer helped the Reds get back into Game 7.

Future Hall of Fame second baseman Joe Morgan's ninth-inning single drove in the winning run in Game 7.

SWEET SOUVENIR
This bottle commemorated the Reds' 1975 World Series win along with the nation's bicentennial when it was sold in 1976.

The Yanks are back

THE TEAM THAT DOMINATED World Series play from the 1920s to early 1960s had not been to the Fall Classic for more than a decade. But in 1976, the Yankees were back. They appeared in three straight Series beginning that year, winning two of them. A new class of heroes emerged, led by Reggie Jackson, "Mr. October." The N.L.'s two Pennsylvania franchises also came through with titles.

Welch later pitched for Oakland and won the 1990 Cy Young Award.

MEET THE YANKS
The Yankees finally thrilled their loyal fans by returning to the Series in 1976. This pass allowed members of the media on the field before the games to interview players.

SPECIAL DAY
This ticket to Game 6 of the 1977 World Series let one lucky fan see one of the most amazing performances in Series history. For details, see "Reggie! Reggie!" below.

12 36B 6
SEC. BOX SEAT

1977 WORLD SERIES

FIELD BOX
Est. Price $13.87
City & St. Tax 1.13
$15.00
YANKEE STADIUM

ADMIT ONE
GAME
6

1977 WORLD SERIES

Yankees

VS.

NATIONAL LEAGUE CHAMPIONS

GAME
6

WHAT A MOMENT!
Bob Welch was a 21-year-old rookie when called into the ninth inning to face superstar Reggie Jackson with Game 2 on the line in 1978. In a classic matchup, the fireballing Welch fanned Jackson on a full count.

RESULTS: 1976–1980
1976 Cincinnati (N.L.) 4, New York (A.L.) 0
1977 New York (A.L.) 4, Los Angeles (N.L.) 2
1978 New York (A.L.) 4, Los Angeles (N.L.) 2
1979 Pittsburgh (N.L.) 4, Baltimore (A.L.) 3
1980 Philadelphia (N.L.) 4, Kansas City (A.L.) 2

75th WORLD SERIES

75 YEARS
This game ball celebrates the 75th anniversary of the first World Series in 1903. The game had grown, but the Fall Classic remained the pinnacle of baseball success.

Players warm up in a batting cage rolled onto the field.

REGGIE! REGGIE!
In Game 6 of the 1977 Series, which the Yankees won to clinch their first title since 1962, New York outfielder Reggie Jackson hit three home runs on three pitches. He was the first player since Babe Ruth to go yard three times in one game.

Dodgers first baseman Steve Garvey

Yankees catcher Thurman Munson

A COUPLE OF LEADERS
Though Thurman Munson was out on this play in the 1978 World Series, he was a huge part of the Yankees' second straight World Series title. The team captain, he provided fiery leadership and a solid bat. Sadly, Munson was killed in a plane crash during the 1979 season.

PINNING ON ONE
By this time, ceramic, or cloisonne pins were becoming popular souvenirs at many sporting events. Companies, teams, leagues, and others created pins. This one commemorates the Yankees' 1978 World Series appearance, topped by the team's familar red, white, and blue top hat.

Pin shows Yankee Stadium's famous facade

SERIES STAR AND FUTURE MANAGER
Fiery outfielder Lou Piniella played in all six of the Yankees' games in 1978 Series. His four RBI were among those that helped the Bronx Bombers become the first team to lose the first two games of a Series and then come back to win it all in six games. Piniella later became a manager with several teams.

THEY WERE FAM-I-LEE
Rockin' out to the popular song "We Are Family," the Pittsburgh Pirates won the 1979 World Series behind the slugging of inspirational team captain Willie Stargell, who had three homers and seven RBI.

The Pirates were among the first teams to wear one-color uniforms that were a color other than white or gray.

FINALLY...THE PHILLIES
Philadelphia third baseman Mike Schmidt was perhaps the best ever at his position. With 10 Gold Gloves and more than 500 homers, he put together one of the greatest careers of his era. He was missing one thing, however: a World Series ring. He wasn't the only one; the Phillies had never won a World Series and hadn't even appeared in one since 1950. In 1980, everyone got what they wanted as the Phillies stormed to a Series title, knocking off Baltimore in six games.

Schmidt batted .381 with two homers and seven RBI in the Series.

Stirrup socks of this time were very thin, compared to those of earlier years.

Five Series of stories

THE EARLY 1980S SAW an interesting mix of teams carry home the World Series trophy. Each season had a unique story that captured the attention of baseball fans. In 1981, the big story was Fernando Valenzuela, while in 1982 the Brewers made their first appearance. The 1983 Series saw the emergence of Cal Ripken, Jr., while the Tigers' 1984 dominance was one for the record books. In 1985, a Series featuring two Missouri teams was called the I-70 Series.

Cardinals second baseman Tommy Herr

CARDINALS FLY
If not for the Yankees, the Cardinals would be baseball's all-time champs. Their seven-game win over Milwaukee in the 1982 Series was their ninth overall, second only to the Yankees.

FERNANDOMANIA!
Out of nowhere, Fernando Valenzuela won the 1981 Cy Young and Rookie of the Year awards, the first player ever to do so. He kept it up in the World Series, winning Game 3 as the Dodgers beat the Yanks in the 11th Series meeting of the two teams.

Milwaukee outfielder Ben Oglivie

YOUNG SUCCESS
The Milwaukee Braves had left for Atlanta in 1965, but the Brewers became an expansion team there in 1970. A dozen years later, they treated their fans to a World Series trip. This pennant was printed up a bit too early, though!

WORLD CHAMPIONS 1982

Outfielder Dan Ford

BIG SHOW IN BALTIMORE
Shortstop Cal Ripken, Jr., the 1983 A.L. MVP, was not exactly a star in the World Series (batting .167), but he and his teammates knocked off the Phillies to claim the first title for Baltimore since 1970.

The Tigers' logo is a capital D written in an "Old English" style.

TIGERS ROAR IN '84
The Detroit Tigers got off to a roaring start in 1984, winning 35 of their first 40 games. They rolled through the playoffs and then smashed the San Diego Padres in the World Series, completing a season of dominant play matched by few teams.

Relief ace Willie Hernandez won the A.L. Cy Young and MVP awards in 1984 and had two saves in the World Series.

RESULTS: 1981–1985

1981 Los Angeles (N.L.) 4, New York (A.L.) 2

1982 St. Louis (N.L.) 4, Milwaukee (A.L.) 3

1983 Baltimore (A.L.) 4, Philadelphia (N.L.) 1

1984 Detroit (A.L.) 4, San Diego (N.L.) 1

1985 Kansas City (A.L.) 4, St. Louis (N.L.) 3

ALMOST A HERO
Lefty pitcher John Tudor won Games 1 and 4 for St. Louis in 1985, but his rocky start led to an 11–0 pasting by the Royals in the deciding Game 7.

Cardinal logo shows two birds perched on a baseball bat.

KIRK CRUSHES
Former football hero Kirk Gibson crushed two homers in Game 5 of the 1984 Series, giving the Tigers all the runs they needed to complete their super season.

Gibson was an All-America wide receiver at Michigan State.

1982 World Champions

Coke and Cardinals #1

SERIES SODA
After the Cards won the 1982 World Series, Coca-Cola issued its product in these special bottles. The back had the score of all the Series games printed on it. Like the Bicentennial bottle on page 33, this unopened bottle of what is now probably very flat soda was saved for posterity.

DREAM SEASON ENDS WITH A BANG
The 1985 season was a dream come true for Kansas City pitcher Bret Saberhagen (31). In only his second pro season, he won 20 games and the A.L. Cy Young Award. In the World Series, he won two games, pitching a shutout in Game 7, to win the World Series MVP trophy, too. He leaped into the arms of future Hall of Fame third baseman George Brett as the final out was made.

Ball autographed on the sweet spot

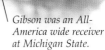

BALL SIGNED BY BYE-BYE
Kansas City's slugging first baseman sported one of the best baseball nicknames. Steve "Bye-Bye" Balboni was known for his long home runs (he hit 36 while helping the Royals to the 1985 title) and his strikeouts (he had 166 that season). He signed this ball for a fan after his career was over.

A Mets miracle

ONCE AGAIN, THE RED SOX found themselves involved in a thrilling, historic World Series in 1986. Unfortunately, as had happened in 1946 and again in 1975, Boston also found itself going home once again without a championship as fate intervened to cloud their chances. As in 1975, Boston was in a position to win it all but let ultimate victory slip (almost literally, it turned out) through their fingers. Only one strike away from beating the New York Mets in Game 6 and winning the World Series (for what would have been the first time since 1918), Boston let the Mets tie the score on a wild pitch and win the game on an error by normally reliable first baseman Bill Buckner. The Sox also had a chance to win Game 7, but they were foiled once again.

GOOD KNIGHT
Surprise World Series star Ray Knight wore this batting helmet while batting .391 with a homer and five RBI. Knight scored the winning run in the famous Game 6.

PAINT THE BLACK
Members of the Mets' Series winning team signed this home plate. Note that it's not an official MLB home plate, which is all white. But this souvenir model is perfect for collecting autographs.

Rocket-armed Boston outfielder Dwight Evans had two homers in this Series.

CHAMPIONSHIP RIDE
How memorable was 1986 for Mets fans? When the RC Ertl company decided to put out a set of toy cars commemorating various baseball events, they chose the 1986 Mets as one of the first teams to honor. The 12-inch-long car is decorated with team logos and the official World Series logo on the back window.

CANCELING INSURANCE
New York's Gary Carter lays the tag on a sliding Jim Rice of the Red Sox during the seventh inning of the pivotal Game 6. Had Rice scored, the Red Sox would have taken a four-run lead that might have been enough to win.

ALMOST A HERO
Boston outfielder Dwight Evans was nearly an eternal hero to Red Sox fans. In Game 7, his leadoff homer in the second inning scored the first run of the game, and his two-run double in the eighth helped Boston close the gap. But in the end, his heroics were not enough and the Mets won Game 7 8–5.

Jim Rice of Boston had 10 hits and a .333 average in the seven-game Series.

New York Mets

1986 POST SEASON MEDIA GUIDE

1962 · Mets · 1986
25th
ANNIVERSARY

ANNIVERSARY EDITION
For every World Series, each team and Major League Baseball prepare special guides for the media, listing all the information and stats that writers and reporters can use in describing the games to fans around the world.

BOSTON'S ACE
Boston lefty Bruce Hurst was the pitching star for the team, winning two games. He left Game 7 with the scored tied 3–3.

UNFAIRLY, A GOAT
Bill Buckner's error allowed the winning run to score in Game 6, but most fans forget that the game was tied and that the Sox had a chance to win in Game 7. Buckner's great career was sadly tarnished by his mistake.

Hurst pitched a shutout to win Game 1.

CAN YOU BELIEVE IT?
The other story of the 1986 Series, after the Red Sox' stunning collapse, is the awesome comeback by a gritty Mets team that was down to its last strike but came back to win—and then celebrate on the infield.

Catcher Gary Carter led the Mets with nine RBI.

Series surprises

MORE OFTEN THAN NOT, teams expected to do well in the regular season do just that and advance to the World Series. But this quartet of Fall Classics each featured a surprise, though some were more serious than others. In 1987, the unheralded Twins surprised everyone by winning. In 1988, gimpy Dodgers' pinch-hitter Kirk Gibson homered to win Game 1 and knock the mighty A's off their stride. In 1989, a tragic earthquake forced the Series to pause for more than a week. And in 1990, a Reds team pulled off perhaps the biggest Series upset in decades.

Sport magazine named Viola the MVP in '87

WINNING WHITE FLAG
During games at the Twins' indoor ballpark, the Metrodome, fans waved Homer Hankies like this one to create a blizzard of white in the stands.

GOLD FOR FRANKIE V.
Viola's heroics on the mound earned him the World Series Most Valuable Player award.

Manager Tom Kelly's signature

SURPRISE STAR
Mickey Hatcher was so surprised when he hit a homer in Game 1 that he sprinted around the bases. He wasn't the only one; Hatcher had had only one homer all season and went on to have two in the five-game Series. Timing, as always, is everything.

WINNERS WRITE
All the members of the Twins' 1987 championship team inscribed this ball. Balls such as this are prized by collectors as a handy way to gather a large number of autographs.

Viola went 17–10 with a 2.90 ERA for the 1987 Twins.

ACE IN '87
Twins lefthander Frank Viola opened the Series with a victory in Game 1. He came back in Game 7 with eight strong innings to clinch the Series. He allowed only three walks in 19.1 innings.

BULLDOG
Orel Hershiser continued an amazing 1988 season by winning two games and the World Series MVP trophy, leading the Dodgers over the A's in five games.

Earlier in 1988, Hershiser set a record with 59 consecutive scoreless innings.

WHAT A MOMENT!
This ticket is from Game 1 of the 1988 Series, which an injured Kirk Gibson won with a two-run, game-winning pinch homer off Oakland ace Dennis Eckersley. It was one of the most famous homers of all time.

RESULTS: 1987–1990

1987 Minnesota (A.L.) 4, St. Louis (N.L.) 3

1988 Los Angeles (N.L.) 4, Oakland (A.L.) 1

1989 Oakland (A.L.) 4, San Francisco (N.L.) 0

1990 Cincinnati (N.L.) 4, Oakland (A.L.) 0

PUNCH UP A WINNER
Al Clark makes the call, Bret Butler and the Giants are out of time, and Dennis Eckersley of the A's starts the celebration as Oakland wins the Bay Area Series in four games over the Giants. Eckersley earned a save in the game.

Eckerseley earned his only save of the Series in this Game 4 victory.

SUDDENLY, THE SERIES STOPPED
As fans and players gathered at San Francisco's Candlestick Park for Game 3 of the 1989 Series, a large earthquake struck the area. The stadium shook, frightening everyone. As this cover of *Sports Illustrated* shows, players pulled families to the safety of the field as a live TV audience watched in shock. The quake caused more than 60 deaths and billions of dollars in damage. The Series was postponed for 10 days out of respect for the victims.

RED STORM
Few experts gave the rather ho-hum lineup of the Cincinnati Reds much of a chance against an A's team that boasted two 20-game winners, the Cy Young-winning Dennis Eckersley, stolen base king Rickey Henderson, and sluggers Mark McGwire and Jose Canseco. Yet the Reds won in a stunning sweep—that's why they play the games!

Catcher Joe Oliver had a game-winning hit in Game 2.

Well known for his plastic goggles, Chris Sabo had two homers in the Series.

Nail-biters in '91

THOUGH THE WORLD SERIES always features the best teams from each league, the Series itself is not always a classic. That was not the case in 1991, however, as the Twins and Braves battled in what many regard as the greatest overall Series ever. Five of the games were decided by only one run; three went to extra innings. The Twins won the last two games at home in their final at-bats. And Game 7 itself featured fantastic pitching, timely hitting, and some very memorable plays.

This Series was truly a Fall Classic.

KIRBY'S GOLD
Minnesota's popular outfielder Kirby Puckett earned this ring for helping the Twins win the Series.

Commissioner Fay Vincent signed this ball to prove its authenticity.

BRINGING HOME THE HARDWARE
In a crowded Minnesota locker room, Twins manager Tom Kelly (left) and owner Carl Pohlad hoisted the World Series trophy.

A HISTORIC BASEBALL
Twins outfielder Gene Larkin hit this ball to win Game 7 of the Series. After important events such as this, representatives of the Hall of Fame request objects like this ball, which are then displayed at the Hall in Cooperstown, New York.

Catchers' chest protectors and shin guards help protect them during home-plate collisions.

Final Out field Hit Gene Larkin to LF Game 7 10/27/91 Fay Vincent

GAME 7 ACE
Twins pitcher Jack Morris pitched all 10 innings of the Twins' thrilling Game 7 victory for his second win in the Series.

THE SERIES WINNER
In the bottom of the 10th inning of Game 7, with the score tied 0–0, the Twins had loaded the bases with one out. With the Braves' outfield pulled in, outfielder Gene Larkin whacked a pitch over the left fielder's head, allowing Dan Gladden to score the World Series-winning run.

SMACKDOWN
In Game 1, Minnesota's Dan Gladden tried to score, but Braves catcher Greg Olson held on to the ball. The collision sent Olson tumbling heels-over-head, and photographer Rich Pilling of MLB Photos captured the moment in this famous photo.

Protective plastic shin guard

42

Lemke played in a total of four World Series for Atlanta in the 1990s.

The righthanded Puckett's helmet had an earflap on the left side only.

SURPRISE SERIES STAR
It happens more than you might think. A light-hitting player comes into the Series and is suddenly a star. Braves second baseman Mark Lemke hit .234 in the season, but .417 in the Series with four RBI.

IT WAS TIME FOR A HERO
In Game 6, Kirby Puckett electrified the home fans with two great plays. First, his great catch took a homer away from Atlanta's Ron Gant. Then, in the bottom of the 11th, he snapped a 3–3 tie and won the game with a dramatic home run. Here he charges around the bases after that hit.

GATE SEC ROW SEAT
F 131 11 3

BOX
$60.00

GAME
2

HHH METRODOME

1991

WORLD SERIES
AMERICAN LEAGUE
VS
NATIONAL LEAGUE

MINNESOTA
Twins

VS.

NATIONAL LEAGUE
CHAMPIONS

1991
World Series

FALL CLASSIC

RAIN CHECK

RAIN CHECK subject to the conditions
set forth on back hereof
DO NOT DETACH THIS COUPON
FRANCIS T. VINCENT, JR.
Commissioner of Baseball

GAME
2

Signed by a pair of Series visitors — Hall of Famers Lou Brock and Willie Stargell

CELEBRATING THE CHAMPS
This pennant honors the Twins' second A.L. title in five years. They returned to the Series in 1991 after finishing last in 1990.

AMERICAN LEAGUE CHAMPIONS

MINNESOTA Twins

1991 World Series

THANKS, FANS
The Twins home park at the Metrodome gave them a real advantage in this tight Series. Packing more than 55,000 people into the indoor arena, the team enjoyed very, very loud support. A fan used this ticket to watch the home team win Game 1 5–2.

PILE UP AT HOME PLATE
Time to celebrate! The Twins surround Dan Gladden after he scores the winning run to end the 1991 World Series. While most players joined in this dancing group, others started looking toward first base, where Gene Larkin, who had driven in Gladden, was waiting.

Baseball's ups and downs

Following the thrills of the 1991 Series, and the stunning ending of the 1993 Series, baseball would soon plummet to one of the lowest points in its history. Due to a labor dispute between players and owners, the 1994 season ceased play in August. For the first time since 1904, the World Series was not played. But the sport and the Series returned; old faces (the Braves) returned to the Fall Classic, while new stars (the expansion Marlins) hoisted the Series trophy.

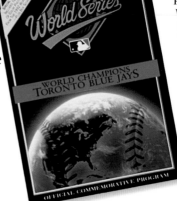

HONORING THE CHAMPS
World Series programs are always collector's items. After the Blue Jays won in 1992, this special edition of the World Series program was issued with the complete story of the team's victory added to the issue.

O CANADA!
The Toronto Blue Jays became the second Canadian franchise when they joined the A.L. in 1977. (The Montreal Expos joined the N.L. in 1969.) The Jays were the first Canadian team to win a Series, in 1992.

BRING ON THE HARDWARE
Rickey Henderson had already won a World Series with Oakland in 1988. After helping Joe Carter (right) hoist the 1993 World Series title, the Majors' all-time leader in stolen bases and runs added another ring to his collection of honors. Henderson had been brought over to Toronto midway through the season; his veteran leadership and leadoff sparkplug played a big part in the Jays' win.

O HAPPY JAY
For only the second time in World Series history, the Fall Classic ended with a game-winning home run. In Game 6, Toronto's Joe Carter launched a pitch from Philadelphia reliever Mitch "The Wild Thing" Williams into the left-field seats for a three-run homer. It won the game 8–6 and the Series and set off Carter's joyous, leaping, shouting celebration.

The Blue Jays were named as the result of a newspaper contest.

RESULTS: 1992–1997

1992	Toronto (A.L.) 4, Atlanta (N.L.) 2
1993	Toronto (A.L.) 4, Philadelphia (N.L.) 2
1994	No World Series played.
1995	Atlanta (N.L.) 4, Cleveland (A.L.) 2
1996	New York (A.L.) 4, Atlanta (N.L.) 2
1997	Florida (N.L.) 4, Cleveland 3 (A.L.)

1994 World Series logo

UNUSED BALL
On September 15, 1994, the sad news came down: The World Series was canceled. The specially imprinted baseballs (above) had already been made, however, and soon became hot collector's items.

NOT THE BILLS
In the NFL, the Buffalo Bills earned a sad reputation when they made it to four straight Super Bowls, only to lose all four. The Braves avoided that fate in 1995 when they defeated the Indians. The Braves had lost in 1992 and would lose again in 1996 and 1999, along with playoff losses in other years in the decade. In 1995 (right), however, they rode the pitching arms of Greg Maddux and Tom Glavine to a six-game triumph over Cleveland.

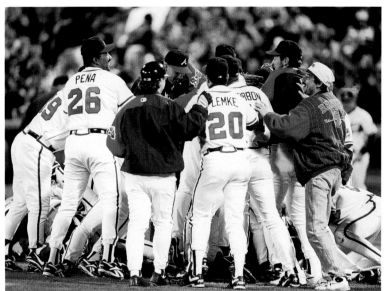

IT'S ABOUT TIME!
Spoiled Yankee fans had watched with sadness for 18 years as their beloved Bronx Bombers failed to win a championship, the longest such drought in team history. But they had new reason to cheer in 1996 when the Yankees won Game 6 at Yankee Stadium. MVP John Wetteland earned his third save in the 3-2 win.

A WILD AND WACKY SERIES
The 1997 Marlins-Indians Series featured the first Series game in Florida history (Game 1 on October 18); a 15-degree windchill in Cleveland for Game 4, the coldest-ever Series game; and an 11-inning Game 7 clincher. When Florida's Craig Counsell (shown fielding here) crossed home plate with the winning run, the five-year-old Marlins became the fastest expansion team ever to win it all.

GOOD EATS
Marlins fans could enjoy a special treat after their team won the World Series in 1997 by diving into this special commemorative box of cereal. The cover shows the team celebrating on the field. It was available in stores shortly after the final game.

Florida second baseman Craig Counsell

Cleveland shortstop Omar Vizquel

VICTORY SHOUT
Florida pitcher Livan Hernandez won two games and earned the 1997 Series MVP award. Hernandez was born in Cuba and played on the national teams there. While on a trip to Mexico, he defected, eventually entering the United States. He signed his first professional contract in the Majors only a year before this Series triumph.

A Yankees sweep

Hoffman had 53 saves in 1998 for San Diego.

The Yankees did it first, the A's did it second, and from 1998 to 2000, the Yankees did it again. What was their feat? Winning three World Series titles in a row. The 1949–1953 Yanks were the first to threepeat. Oakland did it in 1972–1974. In 1998, the Yankees started a new triple play. They knocked off the Padres, Braves, and Mets to match the record. The 2000 Series, in particular, was memorable as a return to the Subway Series of the 1950s among New York teams.

1998 PROGRAM
For Yankees fans, this program represents the beginning of three special years for the Bronx Bombers. They won three straight from 1998–2000.

HOFFMAN CAN'T SAVE SAN DIEGO
In 1998, San Diego boasted one of baseball's best closers in Trevor Hoffman. However, you can only use a closer if you're winning near the end. San Diego was swept in four games by the Yanks and Hoffman saw little action.

VIVA ORLANDO!
The rich got richer when talented Cuban pitcher Orlando Hernandez joined the Yankees for the 1998 season. His high leg kick made it hard for batters to pick up the ball, and his nasty stuff made it simply hard to hit. He won Game 2 of the Series.

Hernandez escaped from Cuba in a boat to head for freedom and baseball glory.

Brosius was named MVP.

JUMP FOR JOY
Yankees third baseman Scott Brosius leaps in the air to begin the celebration of the team's second World Series in three seasons (they also won in 1996). It was a clean four-game win for the Bombers, the first Series sweep since the Reds did it in 1990.

RESULTS: 1998–2000
1998 New York (A.L.) 4, San Diego (N.L.) 0
1999 New York (A.L.) 4, Atlanta (N.L.) 0
2000 New York (A.L.) 4, New York (N.L.) 1

World Series logo

PIN IT ON
San Diego fans had enjoyed only one previous World Series, in 1984, and they got behind their team in 1998 with pins like this one.

TWO IN A ROW
Not even slugging third baseman Chipper Jones' home run swing could keep the Atlanta Braves from becoming the Yankees' second straight sweep victim. Though Jones hit a homer on this swing in Game 1, the Braves as a team batted only .200 in the four-game Series.

SUBWAY SERIES TRADITION
The World Series has been New York vs. New York 14 times. These are always nicknamed "Subway Series" because the city and its ballparks are linked by underground trains.

THE LUCKIEST FANS ON THE FACE OF THE EARTH

NOTHING IS SWEETER THAN JETER

OUCH

Piazza played the bulk of his early career with the Dodgers.

NEW YORK FANS
All of New York City got excited about the 2000 World Series, which pitted two teams from the city for the first time since 1956. This sign echoes the famous words of Yankee great Lou Gehrig from his 1939 farewell speech.

WINNERS AND . . .
Fans flocked to Yankee Stadium (left) and Shea Stadium, home of the Mets (right), though each set of fans ended up with different emotions following the Yankees' five-game victory.

THE MIGHTY MET
Catcher Mike Piazza joined the Mets in 1999 and a year later helped the Mets to their first Series since 1986. Piazza, the best-hitting catcher in baseball history, had a homer and four RBI in a losing cause.

Derek Jeter

Bernie Williams

Luis Sojo

THREE FOR THREE
A trio of Yankees stars celebrates as their team heads toward the second threepeat in franchise history. The Subway Series against the Mets provided great drama, but in the end it was the team from the Bronx, not Queens, that became baseball royalty.

Triumph over tragedy

ONLY A FEW WEEKS BEFORE THE scheduled start of the 2001 World Series, America—and the world—was struck by the horror of the September 11 terrorist attacks on America. The baseball season, like most things, stopped for mourning. But as they have done in many crises past, Americans turned to baseball for solace. The World Series turned into a patriotic affair—with thrilling games!

TWO FOR THE CITY
Two New York heroes got together before the World Series to honor the many heroes from September 11. Yankees manager Joe Torre and New York City mayor Rudolph Giuliani wore special Yankees-themed fire helmets during a special pre-Series rally to honor the team and city firefighters and police.

WORLD SERIES BEANIE BEAR
The Beanie Babies toys were very popular in the late 1990s and early 2000s. Special bears were designed for many events. This red, white, and blue bear for the World Series took on added meaning in the wake of September 11. It was one of dozens of ways that baseball showed its patriotic colors in 2001.

JETER DOES IT AGAIN
Yankees shortstop Derek Jeter has become one of the best World Series clutch hitters ever. In Game 4, after Tino Martinez tied the score with a dramatic homer in the bottom of the ninth, Jeter smacked a two-out homer to right in the bottom of the tenth that won the game for New York. A packed house in Yankee Stadium roared along with Jeter as he ran the bases. Combined with the events of Game 5 (right), this was the most stunning pair of comebacks in Series history.

Score of Game 1 and Gonzalez's stats from that game

DIRTY SOUVENIR
Showing the infield dirt and spike marks of a hard day at the park, this base was used in Game 1 of the Series. Later signed by Arizona's Curt Schilling and Luis Gonzalez (who also signed the ball), this base became a valuable and unique collectible.

BROSIUS MAKES IT TWO IN A ROW
With the baseball world and Yankees fans still reeling from their team's amazing comeback in Game 4, Game 5 proved to be nearly as dramatic. Again down by two runs in the bottom of the ninth, and again facing Arizona reliever Byung-Hyun Kim, the Yanks did it again. This time it was Scott Brosius, whose two-out, two-run homer tied the score. The Yankees eventually won the game in the 12th inning on a single by Alfonso Soriano.

Plastic shin guard protects against foul balls hitting leg or ankle.

Gonzalez drove in Jay Bell from third base; Arizona won 3–2.

ARIZONA MASCOT
Arizona fans were led in their victory cheers by their mascot, BOBCat. His name comes from the nickname of Arizona's home field, Bank One Ballpark, commonly called "The Bob."

Why not a diamondback snake for their mascot? Bobcats are more cuddly!

A BIG LITTLE HIT
Though the Yankees provided the drama in Games 4 and 5, in Game 7, it was Arizona's turn. Down by a run against ace Yankees closer Mariano Rivera, the Diamondbacks rallied. With this hit that squeaked into the outfield, Luis Gonzalez knocked in the Series-winning run.

VALUABLE PAIR
The 2001 World Series produced some thrilling games, and a Series first: two pitchers as co-MVPs. Arizona's Randy Johnson (holding up Commissioner's Trophy) won three games, including Game 7 in relief, and Curt Schilling (far right), who had a 1.69 ERA in three starts, shared the honor.

Brosius's homer set a record. Never before had a team come from behind in the ninth in consecutive Series games.

A heavenly Series

THE ANAHEIM ANGELS, formerly known as the Los Angeles Angels and the California Angels, had never before earned a trip to baseball's most heavenly place: the World Series. But in 2002, they put together one of the most remarkable seasons in recent years and flew home on Angels' wings with the title. To earn it, they had to overcome a great performance by one of the greatest hitters of all time. On the way, they had help from an unlikely—and furry—source.

GOLDEN BALL
Special gold ink was used to put the World Series logo and the signature of Commissioner Bud Selig on this official ball.

Cal Ripken, Jr.   Pete Rose   Hank Aaron   Mark McGwire   Kirk Gibson

SURE AND STEADY
Angels outfielder Garret Anderson had become one of the A.L.'s top RBI men. He proved it in the clutch, knocking in three runs in the team's 4–1 Game 7 win.

A GATHERING OF STARS
Before Game 2 of the Series, Major Leage Baseball honored its Most Memorable Moments. Many of the great heroes who made those moments happen took part in an on-field ceremony. No. 1 was Cal Ripken, Jr., breaking Lou Gehrig's consecutive games-played streak in 1995.

K-ROD MAKES HIS MARK
The World Series can sometimes make folk heroes out of young players. In 2002, the hero was Francisco Rodriguez, the Venezuelan native known as K-Rod for his ability to strike out hitters. Though only a rookie, he shone in the postseason, providing excellent set-up relief work for closer Troy Percival.

Young pitchers often sport high uniform numbers.

Bonds was walked a record 13 times in the Series.

BONDS GOES YARD
Barry Bonds, one of baseball's greatest home-run hitters, had never had a chance at a World Series before. He made the most of it in 2002, hitting four homers, including this enormous blast in his very first Series at-bat.

And a monkey shall lead them

One of the big stories of the 2002 World Series was the help provided by fans of both teams. While Giants fans packed a screaming (and beautiful) PacBell Park, Angels fans set a new standard for noise by banging together pairs of inflated plastic tubes called Thunderstix to cheer their team on. The two-foot-long tubes have since become popular at other sporting events. Two alone don't make much noise, but make it 100,000 of them and you've really got something!

Thunderstix

Velcro holds monkey around neck

Angels third baseman Troy Glaus, the World Series MVP

THE RALLY MONKEY
The other important addition brought by the fans was the Rally Monkey. Originally a short video clip of a real monkey used by the team to encourage the fans to cheer during an Angels comeback, the monkey (stuffed versions are shown above) came to symbolize the team's never-say-die attitude.

ROCKETS' RED GLARE
Fireworks exploded above Edison Field as the improbable World Series champions celebrated the end of a very exciting World Series. The big highlight for the Angels was their stunning comeback in Game 6. Down 5–0 and down to their final eight outs, they somehow managed—with the help of homers from Scott Spiezio and Darin Erstad and a double from Series MVP Troy Glaus (far left)—to rally and overtake the Giants, winning 6–5. It was the first time in Series history a team had come from that far behind to win a game they had to win to keep their Series dreams alive.

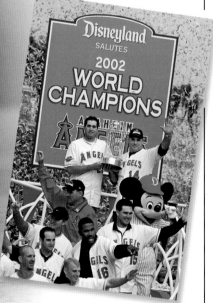

THEY LOVE A PARADE
In 2002, the Angels were owned by the Walt Disney Co., so Disneyland helped put on the Angels' victory celebration, with a little help from Mickey Mouse.

The magic Marlins

Baseball in 2003 was the Year of the Curses, as two teams that had long sought baseball's biggest prize—the Boston Red Sox and the Chicago Cubs—eventually failed to even make it to the World Series, though they came achingly close. In the end, the mighty Yankees once again enjoyed a trip to the Fall Classic. However, when they got there, they ended up facing a determined team led by a wily old manager. The Florida Marlins used outstanding pitching, timely hitting, and some veteran leadership behind the plate to win it all.

Faces painted with Yankees logo

BILLY MARLIN
Florida's mascot will do anything to fire up his team and their fans. Once, Billy Marlin jumped out of an airplane, hoping to parachute into the stadium. Unfortunately, the head of his costume fell off in midair, landing in a swamp. The headless mascot landed safely outside the stadium. In 2003, he rooted the team on to victory.

BRING ON THE FISH!
What a treat for these young fans to be at Yankee Stadium for a World Series game. Before the game, they had their balls, program, and pens ready to try to get autographs from their favorite players. Unfortunately, the hometown team couldn't please their fans, losing their second Series in three years.

BEHIND AND AT THE PLATE
Ivan Rodriguez certainly was a key part of the Marlins' success, thanks to his work behind the plate (at right). He guided Marlins pitchers to several solid outings, notably Josh Beckett's complete-game shutout in Game 6. Ivan also contributed at the plate, with several key RBI in the playoffs and a .273 average in the World Series.

Andy Pettitte won four games in six World Series.

ACE LEFTY
Lefthander Andy Pettitte was a big part of the Yankees' great run from 1996 to 2003. Against the Marlins, he won Game 2 6–1, but lost in Game 6, 2–0. His 0.57 ERA was best among all starters during the 2003 Series.

READY TO WEAR

Complete with Marlins logo and a patch of the World Series trophy, this World Champion hat was ready for players to wear as the last out was recorded. Hats are made for both teams just in case. The 2003 Yankees "champion" hats were given to charity.

Marlins logo

The coin has no monetary value but might be worth more someday to a collector.

SOUVENIR COIN
Among the many ways that fans can remember a World Series is this limited-edition collectible gold coin, specially struck with the World Series logo.

WHAT A PLAY!
In the fifth inning of a scoreless Game 6, Florida shortstop Alex Gonzalez made a fantastic slide to score the game's first run after Luis Castillo hit a 0–2 single to left. New York's Karim Garcia came up throwing, but Gonzalez reached around Yankees catcher Jorge Posada to scrape home plate with his fingers. Josh Beckett made the run stand up, and Florida won the game and the Series.

BOBBLY SOUVENIR
Talk about a cool collectible! This bobble-head doll of Ivan Rodriguez comes complete with a mini version of the World Series trophy!

A.L. Division Series

In 1995, BASEBALL EXPANDED THE PLAYOFFS. Each league changed from two to three divisions. The winners of each division and a new "wild card" team made it to the postseason. The wild card was the second-place team in each league with the best overall record. The new round of playoffs provided new thrills for baseball fans as more teams had a shot at the postseason. Two best-of-five Division Series are held each year in each league. You can see complete results of all the A.L. and N.L. Division Series on page 68.

Catcher Sandy Alomar, Jr.

THE WRIGHT STUFF
Sometimes a short series of games like a Division Series can make stars of players who seemingly come out of nowhere. That was the case in 1997, when 23-year-old pitcher Jaret Wright beat the Yankees twice to help the Indians win their first ALDS.

Wright won only eight games in 1997.

GRIFFEY LEADS THE M'S IN 1995
The Seattle Mariners, led by superstar Ken Griffey, Jr.'s five homers in five games, surprised the New York Yankees in the first A.L. Division Series. The Yankees won the first two games (including a thrilling 15-inning Game 2), but Seattle won the next two. In the deciding Game 5 at Seattle, Griffey scored the dramatic winning run in the bottom of the eleventh to cap an amazing comeback victory.

Like many Major Leaguers, Rodriguez wore nylon and leather batting gloves on each hand.

MARTINEZ MOUND MAGIC
Following up an incredible Cy Young season, Pedro Martinez set a new standard in the 1999 ALDS. He was injured while starting Game 1. With Boston tied 8–8 in Game 5, Martinez magically recovered. He came on to pitch six scoreless innings in relief, while Boston scored four runs to earn a 12–8 win and their first ALDS victory.

In 1999, Martinez led the A.L. in wins, ERA, and strikeouts.

A-ROD LEADS THE M'S
The departure of Ken Griffey, Jr., for the 2000 season (he was traded to the Reds) left shortstop Alex Rodriguez "the man" in Seattle. A-Rod led the Mariners back to the ALCS, where they easily swamped the Chicago White Sox, who were making their only ALDS appearance. Rodriguez hit .308 in the three-game sweep.

Edgar Martinez is one of the most successful designated hitters of all time.

2000 MARTINEZ SUCCESS
While A-Rod was the star in 2000, that honor fell to designated hitter Edgar Martinez in the 2001 ALDS, when Seattle faced Cleveland. After batting .364 in 2000, Martinez hit .312 in 2001, but contributed two homers and five RBI. Seattle fell behind two games to one after Cleveland's 17–2 rout in Game 3, but strong pitching from Freddy Garcia and Jamie Moyer, plus Martinez's bat, led Seattle to victory.

HE CAME THROUGH
Things were not looking good for the Red Sox against the A's during the 2003 ALDS. Oakland had won the first two games, but the Red Sox had won the next two. In the deciding Game 5 at Oakland, the Red Sox trailed. But slugger Manny Ramirez, with two men on, smashed a homer that proved to be the game winner. He pointed to his teammates (right) as he ran.

Stretchy cotton sweatband

Second baseman Damian Jackson

Both Jackson's and Damon's hats flew off their heads when the players collided.

Centerfielder Johnny Damon

ANOTHER KIND OF FIREWORKS
With an outfield-wall American flag at Oakland Coliseum as a backdrop, a pair of Red Sox players proved that baseball can be a contact sport. During a crucial Game 5 of the 2003 ALDS, Boston's Damian Jackson and Johnny Damon whacked together while chasing a short fly ball. It was a scary moment. But though an ambulance had to take Damon off the field, the players were relatively uninjured. Both took part in the ALCS that followed against the Yankees.

N.L. Division Series

THE ATLANTA BRAVES ARE THE New York Yankees of the N.L. Division Series. The N.L. Division Series have been held every year since 1995, and the Braves took part each year from 1995 to 2003. No other N.L. team has appeared in the postseason for all of those seasons. And even the Yankees can't match the Braves' record of five straight LDS wins (1995–1999). As the stars on these pages show, other teams have also contributed great moments to the short history of the NLDS. The added level of playoffs created in 1995 has expanded the roster of postseason success stories.

NOT EVEN BARRY BONDS . . .
The San Francisco Giants star outfielder could only watch as the World Series-bound Florida Marlins swept his Giants in three games to win an NLDS in 1997. Bonds had only three hits.

OPENING ACE
The key to the Braves' success in the NLDS has been pitching. Greg Maddux won four Cy Young awards with Atlanta. In 1995, he made the first pitch in NLDS history.

A SAN DIEGO BROWN-OUT
Perhaps the best game ever pitched in an NLDS came in 1998, when San Diego's ace righthander Kevin Brown shut down the Houston Astros. In Game 1, he racked up an NLDS-record 17 strikeouts in eight scoreless innings. For the series, he had an amazing 21 strikeouts in only 14 innings.

THE GIANTS GO 0-FOR-2
Though the Giants' Ellis Burks scored on this play from Game 3 of the 2000 NLDS against the Mets, it was the Mets who came out on top. They won this game in 13 innings and then clinched the series in Game 4. It was the Mets' second straight NLDS victory.

Mets catcher Mike Piazza

BRAVES LEAP AHEAD
Braves' catcher Paul Bako was out on this play, but it wasn't enough for Houston, as the Astros lost in their first NLDS appearance in 1997. The Braves' sweep of the 'Stros made it a pair of 3–0 results in the two N.L. Division Series that season.

THE CHICAGO TEASERS
Though confronted with years of frustration, Chicago Cubs fans like this man kept the faith. In 2003, it seemed as if their team would finally do it. Behind the great pitching of Kerry Wood, who won two games, Chicago defeated Atlanta in an NLDS to move one step closer to a World Series—but they lost in a heartbreaking NLCS.

GIANTS SECRET WEAPON
Kenny Lofton gives a low-five to Darren Baker, a Giants batboy in 2002 (and son of then-manager Dusty Baker). Darren was only four, and earned almost as much media attention as the team. For his part, Lofton led the Giants with a .350 average as they beat the Braves.

Patch honoring Marlins' 10th anniversary

SLAM-BANG SERIES ACTION
In one of the most dramatic endings to a postseason game, Marlins catcher Ivan Rodriguez held on to the ball and made the game-ending tag on Giants base runner J.T. Snow, even though Snow crashed into the Gold Glove backstop trying to make him drop the ball. Rodriguez bounced off the ground and triumphantly held up the ball. The big play clinched the win and the series for Florida.

Eason represented thousands of servicemen and -women from Florida.

PROUD MOMENT
You could say that it took an army for the Florida Marlins to beat San Francisco and super-slugger Barry Bonds in 2003. Before Game 3, U.S. Army Specialist Joe Eason threw out the first pitch. Eason was wounded in Operation Iraqi Freedom.

A.L. Championship Series

I n 1969, BASEBALL MADE A BIG CHANGE, adjusting the way each league was organized. For the first time, the American and National Leagues would be split into two "divisions." Previously, the league champion had been the team with the best regular-season record. Now the champions would be determined by a League Championship Series. The winners of each division (East and West) would meet in a best-of-five (later best-of-seven) series to see who would represent their league at the World Series.

BALTIMORE BIG MAN
First baseman Boog Powell's slugging helped the Orioles appear in five of the first six ALCS (1969–1974); they won the first three.

RIVALRIES
The biggest baseball rivalry is between the Red Sox and Yankees. In 1978, they met in a one-game playoff for the A.L. East crown. They also played in the ALCS in 1999 and 2003.

Another A.L. playoff

Only one time before the ALCS began in 1969 was a playoff used to determine the league champion. In 1948, the Boston Red Sox and Cleveland Indians finished the regular season with identical 96–58 records. They were forced into a single winner-take-all game, with the prize being a trip to the World Series. The Indians shut down the mighty Sox and won 8–3.

Jersey signed by Ted Williams

THE KID
Red Sox Hall of Fame outfielder Ted Williams, whose road jersey is shown here, led the A.L. with a .369 average in 1948. But Cleveland manager Lou Boudreau used a special defensive alignment (the Williams Shift) to shut the slugger down in the playoff game.

1948 INDIANS HERO
Hall of Fame pitcher Bob Feller wore this uniform during his career with the Indians. He won 19 games in 1948 to help the Tribe reach the one-game A.L. playoff.

Boston catcher Rich Gedman is too late with the tag.

RUNNING FOR THE DUGOUT
In 1976, Chris Chambliss (center) hit a homer that put the Yankees in the World Series for the first time since 1964. Then he had to battle the fans to make it safely back to the locker room!

COMEBACK EXCITEMENT
The 1986 ALCS was one of the most exciting ever. The California Angels were only one out away from winning their first A.L. pennant when Boston, sparked by Dave Henderson's homer, staged an amazing comeback to win Games 6 and 7.

Wakefield throws almost nothing but knuckleballs.

Aaron Boone is the fourth member of his family to play in the Majors, following grandpa Ray, father Bob, and brother Bret.

WALK-OFF HOMER

The 2003 ALCS ended in most dramatic fashion. After coming back from a three-run deficit against Boston ace Pedro Martinez, the Yankees—perhaps drawing on 75 years of Yankee Stadium magic—won the A.L. pennant on a walk-off homer to lead off the 11th inning. It was hit by third baseman Aaron Boone.

2003 RED SOX PITCHING ACE

If not for Aaron Boone's heroics in Game 7, Red Sox pitcher Tim Wakefield probably would have been the 2003 ALCS MVP. The former outfielder-turned-knuckleball pitcher won Games 1 and 4, baffling the Yankees with his ability to make his knuckler duck, dive, dip, and wobble like a wounded duck.

A CLASSIC RIVALRY

This photograph of Yankees star Derek Jeter sliding in to score while Boston catcher Jason Varitek takes the throw symbolizes the long rivalry between these teams, as well as the great 2003 ALCS they played. Like Jeter scoring here (in Game 2), the Yankees have always barely come out on top in the rivalry, and they did it again in 2003. Though the Red Sox were ahead 5–2 in the bottom of the eighth inning, the Yanks came back to tie the score before Boone's homer won it in the 11th.

Because of their uniforms, the Yankees are sometimes called the Pinstripers.

Red Sox catcher Jason Varitek

Yankees shortstop Derek Jeter

N.L. Championship Series

Unfortunately for the Giants, they lost the 1951 World Series following their dramatic win.

THE BIRTH OF THE N.L. CHAMPIONSHIP SERIES created a new level of competition among some of the oldest and most successful teams. The Reds, Cubs, Braves, and other venerable N.L. teams all have had success (and sorrow) in the NLCS. There have been titanic homers, grand singles, and other one-of-a-kind memories since the first NLCS in 1969.

Other N.L. playoffs

The NLCS began in 1969, but in several previous years, ties at the end of the season forced one- or three-game playoffs to determine a league champ. The most famous came in 1951, when the New York Giants defeated the Brooklyn Dodgers on Bobby Thomson's famous home run in the bottom of the ninth inning of the final game.

HELP FOR THE PRESS
Major League Baseball plays a big part in arranging and running the ALCS and NLCS. The words "working media" mean those members of the press who are writing or broadcasting for deadline; that is, their words will be read or heard right away.

Signed to Sports Immortals Museum by Thomson

HAPPY CAMPERS
Manager Leo Durocher gave outfielder Bobby Thomson a big hug after Thomson's dramatic and memorable 9th-inning homer gave the Giants the N.L. pennant.

FAMOUS FOOTSTEPS
Thanks to the Sports Immortals memorabilia collection, here's a look at the actual home plate that Thomson stepped on after his 1951 homer. It is signed by Thomson (and his Dodgers opponent Duke Snider) and a Giants program is shown from that season as well.

AARON STARTS IT OFF
Atlanta outfielder Hank Aaron, who would become baseball's all-time home run champ in 1974, showed off his specialty during the 1969 NLCS, the first ever. Taking on the Mets, Aaron hit three homers and drove in seven runs. But Hammerin' Hank's heroics were not enough, as the Braves lost to the Mets in three games.

Pete Rose

Bruce Bochy

SMASH-UP IN 1980
Pete Rose and the Phillies didn't let anything get in their way during their NLCS win over the Houston Astros. Here "Charlie Hustle" knocks over Bruce Bochy to score in Game 3.

PADRES PRIDE

The San Diego Padres were born in 1969 but did not earn a spot in the playoffs until 1984. This program is from their first-ever NLCS appearance.

1999'S GRAND SINGLE

Though the Mets lost the 1999 NLCS in six games, Robin Ventura (right) made history by winning Game 5 with a unique hit. With the Mets down 3–2 in the bottom of a rainy 15th inning, he hit a ball out of the stadium with the bases loaded. His joyous teammates didn't let him finish his home-run trot, however. Ventura got a "single" and the Mets won 4–3.

This home run was one of a record eight Bonds hit in the 2002 postseason.

BARRY GOES DEEP

Home-run star Barry Bonds had had little success in the playoffs until 2002. In the NLCS that year, however, he busted out, whacking this home run and adding six RBI as the Giants defeated the Cardinals.

2003 WAS THEIR YEAR

Florida's NLCS MVP Ivan Rodriguez waits to hug pitcher Ugueth Urbina after the Marlins came back to defeat the Cubs, earning the veteran catcher his first trip to the World Series.

Aramis Ramirez of the Cubs watches the Marlins celebrate after Game 6.

2003: NOT THIS YEAR

Once again, the Chicago Cubs ended the season in disappointment as they fell in the NLCS to Florida.

Series ceremonies

ALONG WITH BEING BASEBALL'S championship, the World Series is also baseball's big show. When the Series rolls into the two league-champion cities, it brings along music, pageantry, ceremony, and honors. Before each game, several traditional events are held, from the traditional first pitch ceremony, to the introduction of the teams, to the singing of the national anthem. Trivia time: The anthems of what two countries have been sung before World Series games? Read on for the answer.

During this ceremony, the U.S. flag is never lowered as the other flags are.

BASEBALL BIGWIGS
The World Series brings all of baseball's most important people, on and off the field, together to watch the Fall Classic. The eyes of the world are on the event and all the heavy hitters, with and without bats, attend. In 1923, Yankees owner Jacob Ruppert (right) met with baseball Commissioner Kenesaw Mountain Landis before a Series game.

HONORING AMERICA
Paying tribute to America is part of every baseball game, with the pregame playing or singing of the National Anthem. At World Series games, the ceremonies are often more elaborate, with bands, choirs, superstar performers, and flyovers by military jets. A color guard, as here before a 1998 World Series game in New York, presents the colors. Notice how the American flag never dips as the other flags do.

COUNTRY SONG
The 1992 and 1993 World Series featured a first in ceremonies as the Canadian national anthem, "O Canada," was performed in Canada (here by Michelle Williams in 1992 in Toronto's Skydome) as the Toronto Blue Jays became the first team from outside the U.S. to host (and win) a World Series.

MR. PRESIDENT, PART I
Before most games, a ceremony is held in which a dignitary throws out the first pitch. There's no batter, of course, but it's a time-honored tradition. Here's President Calvin Coolidge doing the honors in 1925 while watching his "hometown" Washington Senators take on the Pittsburgh Pirates.

MEETING OF THE MANAGERS
Before the starting lineups of each World Series team are introduced at the start of the first game at each of the two stadiums, the managers (here Jack McKeon and Joe Torre in 2003) meet at home plate for the traditional pregame handshake. Florida's McKeon became the oldest manager to win a Series.

The bird is named Challenger.

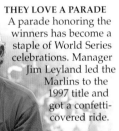

BASEBALL BIRD
A recent entrant, occasionally, at Series pregame ceremonies is this bald eagle, who is trained to fly down into the stadium and land on his handler's leather-covered arm during the playing or singing of the National Anthem.

BASEBALL BOUNCES BACK
Only about a month after the terrible terrorist attacks of September 11, 2001, America turned to baseball and the World Series to help with the healing process. President George W. Bush (himself a former baseball team owner) went to the pitcher's mound in front of 55,000 fans and millions watching on TV to throw out the first ball at Yankee Stadium.

President Bush wore a jacket from the New York City Fire Department.

THEY LOVE A PARADE
A parade honoring the winners has become a staple of World Series celebrations. Manager Jim Leyland led the Marlins to the 1997 title and got a confetti-covered ride.

AVENUE OF CHAMPIONS
For nearly 100 years, a ticker-tape parade through Manhattan's concrete canyons has greeted heroes from aviators to astronauts to presidents. In recent years, fans have also welcomed visits from the New York Yankees, who won four World Series (and got four parades) from 1996 to 2000.

Trophies and rings

THE ULTIMATE GOAL FOR A BASEBALL PLAYER is to win a World Series championship. The ultimate symbol of that triumph, for a player, is the World Series ring. The winning team receives a unique trophy (right), but to the players, "playing for the ring" is the battle cry. Each winning team designs its own rings, using gold, silver, and various jewels. But the rings, though beautiful and valuable, are truly just symbols of the hard work and effort that went into winning.

OLD WS TROPHY
From 1977 to 1997, winning World Series teams received this version of the World Series Championship Trophy. The gold flags on the black ceramic base represent the 30 Major League clubs. A gold crown tops the ring of gold in the center.

Logos of Yankees and their N.L. opponent, the Braves

COMMISSIONER'S TROPHY
In 1998, the World Series trophy was redesigned by Tiffany & Co. Now made of gold and sterling silver, the trophy still includes the traditional pennants of all the teams. It stands 30 inches tall and weighs 30 pounds. But to the team that holds it aloft, it's as light as a feather.

Marlins Lenny Harris, Juan Pierre, and Dontrelle Willis hold the 2003 championship trophy.

TIME TO HOIST THE THE TROPHY
In recent seasons, the World Series trophy has been given to the winning team in a ceremony held on the field immediately following the final out of the final game. The players put on special championship T-shirts and hats and celebrate with the fans. Later, they return to their locker room, as the Marlins show above, and begin a victory party that lasts until spring training starts the following year.

LEAGUE WINNERS
The champions of each league also receive a trophy. This is the N.L. trophy, named for longtime former N.L. president Warren Giles.

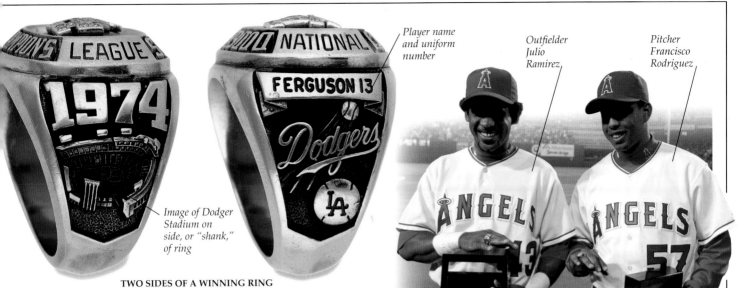

Image of Dodger Stadium on side, or "shank," of ring

Player name and uniform number

Outfielder Julio Ramirez

Pitcher Francisco Rodriguez

TWO SIDES OF A WINNING RING

Some teams issue rings to their players in honor of winning a league championship (usually if they haven't gone on to win a World Series ring). These photos show the two sides of the ring given to Joe Ferguson, an outfielder on the L.A. Dodgers' 1974 N.L.-champion team. Like a World Series ring, it features the year, the player name, the team logo, and other decorations.

IT'S RING TIME!

At a game in the season following their World Series triumph, teams receive their individual World Series rings at a special on-field ceremony, as the Anaheim Angels did in 2003.

The Angels rings took a team of 68 craftspeople more than 30 days to create.

DIAMONDS AND MORE DIAMONDS

While players get the most beautiful and elaborate rings, many other members of a winning team's staff receive a ring as well. This ring was given to scouts for the Yankees' 1996 championship. Like the players' ring, it is made of gold and features the team logo in diamonds on a Yankees-blue background.

BIG HANDS NEEDED

This close-up, enlarged photo of the Anaheim Angels' 2002 World Series championship ring shows just how fancy and beautiful World Series rings have become. A typical man's ring weighs five grams; this ring weighs more than 60 grams! The ring itself is made of 14-karat gold. Each side is cast with various images, including the team logo and the player's name and words noting that this was the team's first World Series championship. Each ring is thus unique and made for one player only. The Angels logo is on the top of the ring and is formed by 15 rubies, surrounded by 57 diamonds. Though valued at $15,000, each of these rings is priceless and one of a kind. And players wouldn't trade them for any amount!

MVPs

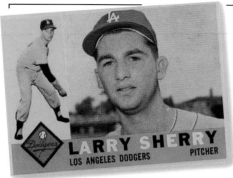

VERSATILE VICTOR
In the Dodgers' 1959 victory over the White Sox, L.A. relief pitcher Larry Sherry had a hand in all four of his team's wins. He had saves in Games 2 and 3 and won Games 4 and 6. He allowed only one run in 12-plus innings.

BASEBALL IS A TEAM GAME, OF COURSE, but individuals do stand out, especially in a short time like a World Series. Beginning in 1955, a Most Valuable Player was named following each World Series. In every case, that MVP has come from the winning team (which makes sense). Twice the award has been shared. In 1981, the Dodgers' Ron Cey, Pedro Guerrero, and Steve Yeager were all co-MVPs. Arizona's Randy Johnson and Curt Schilling split the votes in 2001.

CARDINALS ACE
As the Cardinals won World Series in 1964 and 1967, they depended on the powerful right arm of pitcher Bob Gibson. The hard-throwing pitcher won five games with an incredible 57 strikeouts in the two Series.

1980S HARDWARE
In the 1980s, car company Chevrolet, along with *Sport* magazine, sponsored the MVP award, giving the winner this silver trophy (Bret Saberhagen's 1985 cup is shown at left). After the Series, the winners were flown to New York to get their award at *Sport*'s offices.

MAJOR LEAGUE BASEBALL
CHEVROLET

WORLD SERIES
MOST VALUABLE PLAYER
1985

Porter was one of the few players to wear eyeglasses on the field.

MVP SURPRISE
In many cases, the player who becomes the World Series MVP is not the superstar or the big-name player. Such was the case in 1982 when catcher Darrell Porter was the MVP with a homer and five RBI. It was especially sweet for Porter, who had had a poor regular season.

THE FRUITS OF SUCCESS
In 1984, the Detroit Tigers were wire-to-wire champions. They exploded out of the gate with 35 wins in their first 40 games. A key part of their success was shortstop Alan Trammell. In the World Series, Trammell had two homers and six RBI and batted .450. His feats earned him the MVP award and the keys to this new car!

Trammell drove home a new Pontiac Firebird Trans Am.

LCS MVPs

Beginning in 1977 (N.L.) and 1980 (A.L.), an MVP has been named for each League Championship Series. Though not as prized as the World Series MVP award, the LCS MVP can signal the arrival of a new star or confirmation of a superstar's ability to lead.

RARE MVP FEAT
In 1982, Angels outfielder Fred Lynn became the only player from a losing team to earn an LCS MVP award.

FAMOUS FISH
Catcher Ivan Rodriguez smacked six RBI in 2003 to win the NLCS MVP for the Marlins.

ANDY'S AWARD
Yankees pitcher Andy Pettitte displays his 2003 ALCS MVP award, which he earned by winning two games over the Red Sox.

Trophy made of crystal spires

THE LATEST YANKEES HERO
Derek Jeter has been a big part of the Yankees' recent World Series success. From 1996 to 2003, the shortstop helped the team win four Series titles and six A.L. pennants. In the 2000 Subway Series against the Mets, Jeter hit .409 to become the first player to be the World Series and All-Star Game MVP in the same year.

Josh Beckett had never pitched a complete game as a pro pitcher before he pitched two in the 2003 postseason.

BECKETT BRINGS THE HEAT
Facing the New York Yankees can be intimidating for any young pitcher. Facing the mighty Bronx Bombers in the World Series, at Yankee Stadium, with the World Series on the line? Well, that would make Superman sweat. But not Marlins righthander Josh Beckett. Appearing to be unmoved by the pressure of the moment, Beckett pitched a complete-game shutout in Game 6 of the 2003 Series, in front of a roaring Yankee Stadium crowd, to clinch the championship for the unheralded Marlins. The win, along with his triumph in Game 2, made Beckett the Series MVP and the latest baseball hero to be born in the hot, pressure-packed fires of the Fall Classic.

Appendix
World Series Results

2003	Florida (N.L.) 4, New York (A.L.) 2
2002	Anaheim (A.L.) 4, San Francisco (N.L.) 3
2001	Arizona (N.L.) 4, New York (A.L.) 3
2000	New York (A.L.) 4, New York (N.L.) 1
1999	New York (A.L.) 4, Atlanta (N.L.) 0
1998	New York (A.L.) 4, San Diego (N.L.) 0
1997	Florida (N.L.) 4, Cleveland (A.L.) 3
1996	New York (A.L.) 4, Atlanta (N.L.) 2
1995	Atlanta (N.L.) 4, Cleveland (A.L.) 2
1994	No World Series
1993	Toronto (A.L.) 4, Philadelphia (N.L.) 2
1992	Toronto (A.L.) 4, Atlanta (N.L.) 2
1991	Minnesota (A.L.) 4, Atlanta (N.L.) 3
1990	Cincinnati (N.L.) 4, Oakland (A.L.) 0
1989	Oakland (A.L.) 4, San Francisco (N.L.) 0
1988	Los Angeles (N.L.) 4, Oakland (A.L.) 1
1987	Minnesota (A.L.) 4, St. Louis (N.L.) 3
1986	New York (N.L.) 4, Boston (A.L.) 3
1985	Kansas City (A.L.) 4, St. Louis (N.L.) 3
1984	Detroit (A.L.) 4, San Diego (N.L.) 1
1983	Baltimore (A.L.) 4, Philadelphia (N.L.) 1
1982	St. Louis (N.L.) 4, Milwaukee (A.L.) 3
1981	Los Angeles (N.L.) 4, New York (A.L.) 2
1980	Philadelphia (N.L.) 4, Kansas City (A.L.) 2
1979	Pittsburgh (N.L.) 4, Baltimore (A.L.) 3
1978	New York (A.L.) 4, Los Angeles (N.L.) 2
1977	New York (A.L.) 4, Los Angeles (N.L.) 2
1976	Cincinnati (N.L.) 4, New York (A.L.) 0
1975	Cincinnati (N.L.) 4, Boston (A.L.) 3
1974	Oakland (A.L.) 4, Los Angeles (N.L.) 1
1973	Oakland (A.L.) 4, New York (N.L.) 3
1972	Oakland (A.L.) 4, Cincinnati (N.L.) 3
1971	Pittsburgh (N.L.) 4, Baltimore (A.L.) 3
1970	Baltimore (A.L.) 4, Cincinnati (N.L.) 1
1969	New York (N.L.) 4, Baltimore (A.L.) 1
1968	Detroit (A.L.) 4, St. Louis (N.L.) 3
1967	St. Louis (N.L.) 4, Boston (A.L.) 3
1966	Baltimore (A.L.) 4, Los Angeles (N.L.) 0
1965	Los Angeles (N.L.) 4, Minnesota (A.L.) 3
1964	St. Louis (N.L.) 4, New York (A.L.) 3
1963	Los Angeles (N.L.) 4, New York (A.L.) 0
1962	New York (A.L.) 4, San Francisco (N.L.) 3
1961	New York (A.L.) 4, Cincinnati (N.L.) 1
1960	Pittsburgh (N.L.) 4, New York (A.L.) 3
1959	Los Angeles (N.L.) 4, Chicago (A.L.) 2
1958	New York (A.L.) 4, Milwaukee (N.L.) 3
1957	Milwaukee (N.L.) 4, New York (A.L.) 3
1956	New York (A.L.) 4, Brooklyn (N.L.) 3
1955	Brooklyn (N.L.) 4, New York (A.L.) 3
1954	New York (N.L.) 4, Cleveland (A.L.) 0
1953	New York (A.L.) 4, Brooklyn (N.L.) 2
1952	New York (A.L.) 4, Brooklyn (N.L.) 3
1951	New York (A.L.) 4, New York (N.L.) 2
1950	New York (A.L.) 4, Philadelphia (N.L.) 0
1949	New York (A.L.) 4, Brooklyn (N.L.) 1
1948	Cleveland (A.L.) 4, Boston (N.L.) 2
1947	New York (A.L.) 4, Brooklyn (N.L.) 3
1946	St. Louis (N.L.) 4, Boston (A.L.) 3
1945	Detroit (A.L.) 4, Chicago (N.L.) 3
1944	St. Louis (N.L.) 4, St. Louis (A.L.) 2
1943	New York (A.L.) 4, St. Louis (N.L.) 1
1942	St. Louis (N.L.) 4, New York (A.L.) 1
1941	New York (A.L.) 4, Brooklyn (N.L.) 1
1940	Cincinnati (N.L.) 4, Detroit (A.L.) 3
1939	New York (A.L.) 4, Cincinnati (N.L.) 0
1938	New York (A.L.) 4, Chicago (N.L.) 0
1937	New York (A.L.) 4, New York (N.L.) 1
1936	New York (A.L.) 4, New York (N.L.) 2
1935	Detroit (A.L.) 4, Chicago (N.L.) 2
1934	St. Louis (N.L.) 4, Detroit (A.L.) 3
1933	New York (N.L.) 4, Washington (A.L.) 1
1932	New York (A.L.) 4, Chicago (N.L.) 0
1931	St. Louis (N.L.) 4, Philadelphia (A.L.) 3
1930	Philadelphia (A.L.) 4, St. Louis (N.L.) 2
1929	Philadelphia (A.L.) 4, Chicago (N.L.) 1
1928	New York (A.L.) 4, St. Louis (N.L.) 0
1927	New York (A.L.) 4, Pittsburgh (N.L.) 0
1926	St. Louis (N.L.) 4, New York (A.L.) 3
1925	Pittsburgh (N.L.) 4, Washington (A.L.) 3
1924	Washington (A.L.) 4, New York (N.L.) 3
1923	New York (A.L.) 4, New York (N.L.) 2
1922	#New York (N.L.) 4, New York (A.L.) 0
1921	*New York (N.L.) 5, New York (A.L.) 3
1920	*Cleveland (A.L.) 5, Brooklyn (N.L.) 2
1919	*Cincinnati (N.L.) 5, Chicago (A.L.) 3
1918	Boston (A.L.) 4, Chicago (N.L.) 2
1917	Chicago (A.L.) 4, New York (N.L.) 2
1916	Boston (A.L.) 4, Brooklyn (N.L.) 1
1915	Boston (A.L.) 4, Philadelphia (N.L.) 1
1914	Boston (N.L.) 4, Philadelphia (A.L.) 0
1913	Philadelphia (A.L.) 4, New York (N.L.) 1
1912	*Boston (A.L.) 4, New York (N.L.) 3
1911	Philadelphia (A.L.) 4, New York (N.L.) 2
1910	Philadelphia (A.L.) 4, Chicago (N.L.) 1
1909	Pittsburgh (N.L.) 4, Detroit (A.L.) 3
1908	Chicago (N.L.) 4, Detroit (A.L.) 1
1907	#Chicago (N.L.) 4, Detroit (A.L.) 0
1906	Chicago (A.L.) 4, Chicago (N.L.) 2
1905	New York (N.L.) 4, Philadelphia (A.L.) 1
1904	No World Series
1903	*Boston (A.L.) 5, Pittsburgh (N.L.) 3

* Best of nine series.
# One game included a tie called due to darkness.

ALCS Results

The American League Championship Series was a best-of-five series from 1969 to 1984. As of 1985, the ALCS is played in a seven-game format.

2003	New York 4, Boston 3
2002	Anaheim 4, Minnesota 1
2001	New York 4, Seattle 1
2000	New York 4, Seattle 2
1999	New York 4, Boston 1
1998	New York 4, Cleveland 2
1997	Cleveland 4, Baltimore 2
1996	New York 4, Baltimore 1
1995	Cleveland 4, Seattle 2
1994	No postseason play
1993	Toronto 4, Chicago 2
1992	Toronto 4, Oakland 2
1991	Minnesota 4, Toronto 1
1990	Oakland 4, Boston 0
1989	Oakland 4, Toronto 1
1988	Oakland 4, Boston 0
1987	Minnesota 4, Detroit 1
1986	Boston 4, California 3
1985	Kansas City 4, Toronto 3
1984	Detroit 3, Kansas City 0
1983	Baltimore 3, Chicago 1
1982	Milwaukee 3, California 2
1981	New York 3, Oakland 0
1980	Kansas City 3, New York 0
1979	Baltimore 3, California 1
1978	New York 3, Kansas City 1
1977	New York 3, Kansas City 2
1976	New York 3, Kansas City 2
1975	Boston 3, Oakland 0
1974	Oakland 3, Baltimore 1
1973	Oakland 3, Baltimore 2
1972	Oakland 3, Detroit 2
1971	Baltimore 3, Oakland 0
1970	Baltimore 3, Minnesota 0
1969	Baltimore 3, Minnesota 0

NLCS Results

The National League Championship Series was a best-of-five series from 1969 to 1984. As of 1985, the NLCS is played in a seven-game format.

2003	Florida 4, Chicago 3
2002	San Francisco 4, St. Louis 1
2001	Arizona 4, Atlanta 1
2000	New York 4, St. Louis 1
1999	Atlanta 4, New York 2
1998	San Diego 4, Atlanta 2
1997	Florida 4, Atlanta 2
1996	Atlanta 4, St. Louis 3
1995	Atlanta 4, Cincinnati 0
1994	No postseason play
1993	Philadelphia 4, Atlanta 2
1992	Atlanta 4, Pittsburgh 2
1991	Atlanta 4, Pittsburgh 3
1990	Cincinnati 4, Pittsburgh 2
1989	San Francisco 4, Chicago 1
1988	Los Angeles 4, New York 3
1987	St. Louis 4, San Francisco 3
1986	New York 4, Houston 2
1985	St. Louis 4, Los Angeles 2
1984	San Diego 3, Chicago 2
1983	Philadelphia 3, Los Angeles 1
1982	St. Louis 3, Atlanta 0
1981	Los Angeles 3, Montreal 2
1980	Philadelphia 3, Houston 2
1979	Pittsburgh 3, Cincinnati 0
1978	Los Angeles 3, Philadelphia 1
1977	Los Angeles 3, Philadelphia 1
1976	Cincinnati 3, Pittsburgh 0
1975	Cincinnati 3, Pittsburgh 0
1974	Los Angeles 3, Pittsburgh 1
1973	New York 3, Cincinnati 2
1972	Cincinnati 3, Pittsburgh 2
1971	Pittsburgh 3, San Francisco 1
1970	Cincinnati 3, Pittsburgh 0
1969	New York 3, Atlanta 0

ALDS Results

The expansion from two to three divisions in 1995 created the American League Divisional Series.

2003	New York 3, Minnesota 1
	Boston 3, Oakland 2
2002	Anaheim 3, New York 1
	Minnesota 3, Oakland 2
2001	New York 3, Oakland 2
	Seattle 3, Cleveland 2
2000	New York 3, Oakland 2
	Seattle 3, Chicago 0
1999	New York 3, Texas 0
	Boston 3, Cleveland 2
1998	New York 3, Texas 0
	Cleveland 3, Boston 1
1997	Cleveland 3, New York 2
	Baltimore 3, Seattle 1
1996	New York 3, Texas 1
	Baltimore 3, Cleveland 1
1995	Cleveland 3, Boston 0
	Seattle 3, New York 2

NLDS Results

The expansion from two to three divisions in 1995 created the National League Divisional Series.

2003	Florida 3, San Francisco 1
	Chicago 3, Atlanta 2
2002	San Francisco 3, Atlanta 2
	St. Louis 3, Arizona 0
2001	Arizona 3, St. Louis 2
	Atlanta 3, Houston 0
2000	New York 3, San Francisco 1
	St. Louis 3, Atlanta 0
1999	Atlanta 3, Houston 1
	New York 3, Arizona 1
1998	San Diego 3, Houston 1
	Atlanta 3, Chicago 0
1997	Florida 3, San Francisco 0
	Atlanta 3, Houston 0
1996	Atlanta 3, Los Angeles 0
	St. Louis 3, San Diego 0
1995	Atlanta 3, Colorado 1
	Cincinnati 3, Los Angeles 0

World Series Most Valuable Players

From 1955 to 1986, the World Series MVP award was selected by *Sport* magazine, in conjunction with Chevrolet, which usually awarded a Corvette to the winner. Today, a panel of sportswriters (and in recent years, fans, via Internet voting) have chosen the World Series MVP. Trivia time: Bobby Richardson (1960) is the only World Series MVP from the losing team.

2003	Josh Beckett, P, Florida (N.L.)	1979	Willie Stargell, 1B, Pittsburgh (N.L.)
2002	Troy Glaus, 3B, Anaheim (A.L.)	1978	Bucky Dent, SS, New York (A.L.)
2001	Curt Schilling, P/Randy Johnson, P, Arizona (N.L.)	1977	Reggie Jackson, OF, New York (A.L.)
		1976	Johnny Bench, C, Cincinnati (N.L.)
2000	Derek Jeter, SS, New York (A.L.)	1975	Pete Rose, 3B, Cincinnati (N.L.)
1999	Mariano Rivera, P, New York (A.L.)	1974	Rollie Fingers, P, Oakland (A.L.)
1998	Scott Brosius, 3B, New York (A.L.)	1973	Reggie Jackson, OF, Oakland (A.L.)
1997	Livan Hernandez, P, Florida (N.L.)	1972	Gene Tenace, C, Oakland (A.L.)
1996	John Wetteland, P, New York (A.L.)	1971	Roberto Clemente, OF, Pittsburgh (N.L.)
1995	Tom Glavine, P, Atlanta (N.L.)	1970	Brooks Robinson, 3B, Baltimore (A.L.)
1994	No World Series	1969	Donn Clendenon, 1B, New York (N.L.)
1993	Paul Molitor, DH-3B, Toronto (A.L.)	1968	Mickey Lolich, P, Detroit (A.L.)
1992	Pat Borders, C, Toronto (A.L.)	1967	Bob Gibson, P, St. Louis (N.L.)
1991	Jack Morris, P, Minnesota (A.L.)	1966	Frank Robinson, OF, Baltimore (A.L.)
1990	Jose Rijo, P, Cincinnati (N.L.)	1965	Sandy Koufax, P, Los Angeles (N.L.)
1989	Dave Stewart, P, Oakland (A.L.)	1964	Bob Gibson, P, St. Louis (N.L.)
1988	Orel Hershiser, P, Los Angeles (N.L.)	1963	Sandy Koufax, P, Los Angeles (N.L.)
1987	Frank Viola, P, Minnesota (A.L.)	1962	Ralph Terry, P, New York (A.L.)
1986	Ray Knight, 3B, New York (N.L.)	1961	Whitey Ford, P, New York (A.L.)
1985	Bret Saberhagen, P, Kansas City (A.L.)	1960	Bobby Richardson, 2B, New York (A.L.)
1984	Alan Trammell, SS, Detroit (A.L.)	1959	Larry Sherry, P, Los Angeles (N.L.)
1983	Rick Dempsey, C, Baltimore (A.L.)	1958	Bob Turley, P, New York (A.L.)
1982	Darrell Porter, C, St. Louis (N.L.)	1957	Lew Burdette, P, Milwaukee (N.L.)
1981	Pedro Guerrero, OF/Ron Cey, 3B/Steve Yeager, C, Los Angeles (N.L.)	1956	Don Larsen, P, New York (A.L.)
		1955	Johnny Podres, P, Brooklyn (N.L.)
1980	Mike Schmidt, 3B, Philadelphia (N.L.)		

NLCS Results

The first NLCS MVP award was chosen in 1977. Jeffrey Leonard and Mike Scott are the only two honorees from non-winning clubs.

2003	Ivan Rodriguez, C, Florida
2002	Benito Santiago, C, San Francisco
2001	Craig Counsell, 2B, Arizona
2000	Mike Hampton, P, New York
1999	Eddie Perez, C, Atlanta
1998	Sterling Hitchcock, P, San Diego
1997	Livan Hernandez, P, Florida
1996	Javy Lopez, C, Atlanta
1995	Mike Devereaux, OF, Atlanta
1994	No Postseason Play
1993	Curt Schilling, P, Philadelphia
1992	John Smoltz, P, Atlanta
1991	Steve Avery, P, Atlanta
1990	Rob Dibble, P/Randy Myers, P, Cincinnati
1989	Will Clark, 1B, San Francisco
1988	Orel Hershiser, P, Los Angeles
1987	Jeffrey Leonard, OF, San Francisco
1986	Mike Scott, P, Houston
1985	Ozzie Smith, SS, St. Louis
1984	Steve Garvey, 1B, San Diego
1983	Gary Matthews, OF, Philadelphia
1982	Darrell Porter, C, St. Louis
1981	Burt Hooton, P, Los Angeles
1980	Manny Trillo, 2B, Philadelphia
1979	Willie Stargell, 1B, Pittsburgh
1978	Steve Garvey, 1B, Los Angeles
1977	Dusty Baker, OF, Los Angeles

ALCS Most Valuable Players

The ALCS MVP award was not given until 1980, three years after the National League's first NLCS award winner. Fred Lynn is the only player from a losing team to win the ALCS MVP.

2003	Mariano Rivera, P, New York
2002	Adam Kennedy, 2B, Anaheim
2001	Alfonso Soriano, 2B, New York
2000	David Justice, OF, New York
1999	Orlando Hernandez, P, New York
1998	David Wells, P, New York
1997	Marquis Grissom, OF, Cleveland
1996	Bernie Williams, OF, New York
1995	Orel Hershiser, P, Cleveland
1994	No Postseason Play
1993	Dave Stewart, P, Toronto
1992	Roberto Alomar, 2B, Toronto
1991	Kirby Puckett, OF, Minnesota
1990	Dave Stewart, P, Oakland
1989	Rickey Henderson, OF, Oakland
1988	Dennis Eckersley, P, Oakland
1987	Gary Gaetti, 3B, Minnesota
1986	Marty Barrett, 2B, Boston
1985	George Brett, 3B, Kansas City
1984	Kirk Gibson, OF, Detroit
1983	Mike Boddicker, P, Baltimore
1982	Fred Lynn, OF, California
1981	Graig Nettles, 3B, New York
1980	Frank White, 2B, Kansas City

Index

Photo credits

Thanks to Rich Pilling and Paul Cunningham at MLB Photos, as always, for their help. Thanks to Mark Rucker of the Rucker Archive for many of the old pieces of memorabila. The staff at www.mastronet.com, a great sports auction site, provided some very unique photos of valuable artifacts from their auctions.

t: top; b: bottom; c: center; r: right; l: left

AP/Wide World: 22b; 23tl, cl, cr; 25tl; 27c; 30b; 33bc; 45br; 47tr; 50tr; 51br; 54tl, bl; 55tr, bl; 56–57 all except 56tl; 58br; 59b; 60tr.

Ralph Clevenger: 46bl.

Corbis: 12bc; 13cr; 15tl; 20br; 21bl, tl, c; 22cl; 23bl; 24cl, b; 24tr, br, c; 28cr, b; 29tl; 31tc, cr; 32tc, bl; 34tr, bl, br; 35br; 36tl, tr, bl, br; 41tl, b; 48tr; 56tl; 58bl; 59tl, tr; 60bl, br; 61bc; 66cl, cr, b; 67tr (3).

DK Photos (of objects from the author's personal collection): 23cr; 24cr; 26cl, cr, tl; 33br; 34tl, cr; 35tr; 36c; 37tl, bl; 38tr, cr; 40tl, c, br; 43cl, tr; 44c; 45tl; 45bl; 48tl; 51t; 52cr; 53cr, tr; 58tl; 60tl; 61tl; 66tr.

Getty Images: 64tr; 67tl.

Courtesy Intergold, Inc: 65br.

Courtesy Mastronet (www.mastronet.com): 22cr; 27tl; 31tl; 58tr; 65tl (3).

Library of Congress: 9c; 10bc; 14tr.

MLB Photos: 37tc, br; 39tc; 40b; 41tl, cl, bl, tr; 43b; 44b, cl; 45cr, c, b; 46cl; 54cr; 55tl; 61t, bl, br; 64b, br; 65tr.

MLB Photos (by photographer): Paul Cunningham: 47t; 51tr; Stephen Green: 43tl; 54br; Brad Mangin: 47tc; 50br; Rich Pilling 35bl, tl; 37tr; 39b; 47b, tl; 40bl, cr; 42br; 48br; 49tl, tr; 50tl, bl, c; 51tr; 52c; 53tl, c; Ron Vesely: 43tr; 46cr, tr, br; 48bl; 49b; 51bl; 52bl, tl; 67b.

National Baseball Hall of Fame and Library: All photos on 6–7; 8l; 9t, br, bl; 10tl; 12br; 15tr, c, b; 16cl, cr, bc; 17c; 18c, b; 19tr, cr; 20cl; 21tr, br; 22tr; 23tr; 23br; 26b; 38tl; 42c; 48c.

Northeastern University World Series Museum: 8b, c, tr, br.

Courtesy Sports Immortals Inc.: 10cl; 19br; 24tr; 30cr; 58cr, cl; 60c;

Sports Illustrated: 26tr, 27b (Marvin Newman); 29b, 31tr (Walter Iooss, Jr.); 30tr (Herb Scharfman); 31br; 33t; 38bl, 39tr, 53b (John Iacono); 41tr.

Transcendental Graphics: 10cr, bl, br; 11 all; 12t, c, tr, bl; 13c, br, bc, tr; 14tl, cl, br; 14br, tr; 15bl, br, tr; 18tl; 19b, tr; 20tr(4); 21bc; 22tl; 24tl, tr; 28tl, tr; 29bl; 32tr.